For Dear Grams,
on the occasion of
her 86th birthday!!
In honor of your sharp mind,
your never-ending curiosity,
and your interest in the
culinary arts.
With love,
Joan + Ed

KAIKAI ANIANI

A GUIDE TO

BUSH FOODS MARKETS AND CULINARY ARTS

OF PAPUA NEW GUINEA

ROBERT BROWN & ASSOCIATES

KAIKAI ANIANI

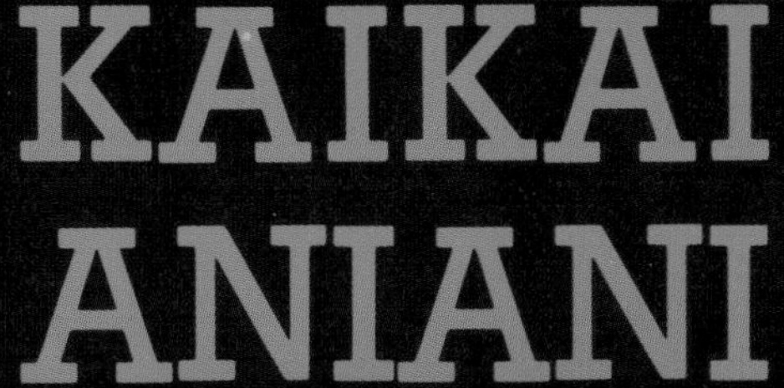

A GUIDE TO

BUSH FOODS MARKETS AND CULINARY ARTS OF PAPUA NEW GUINEA

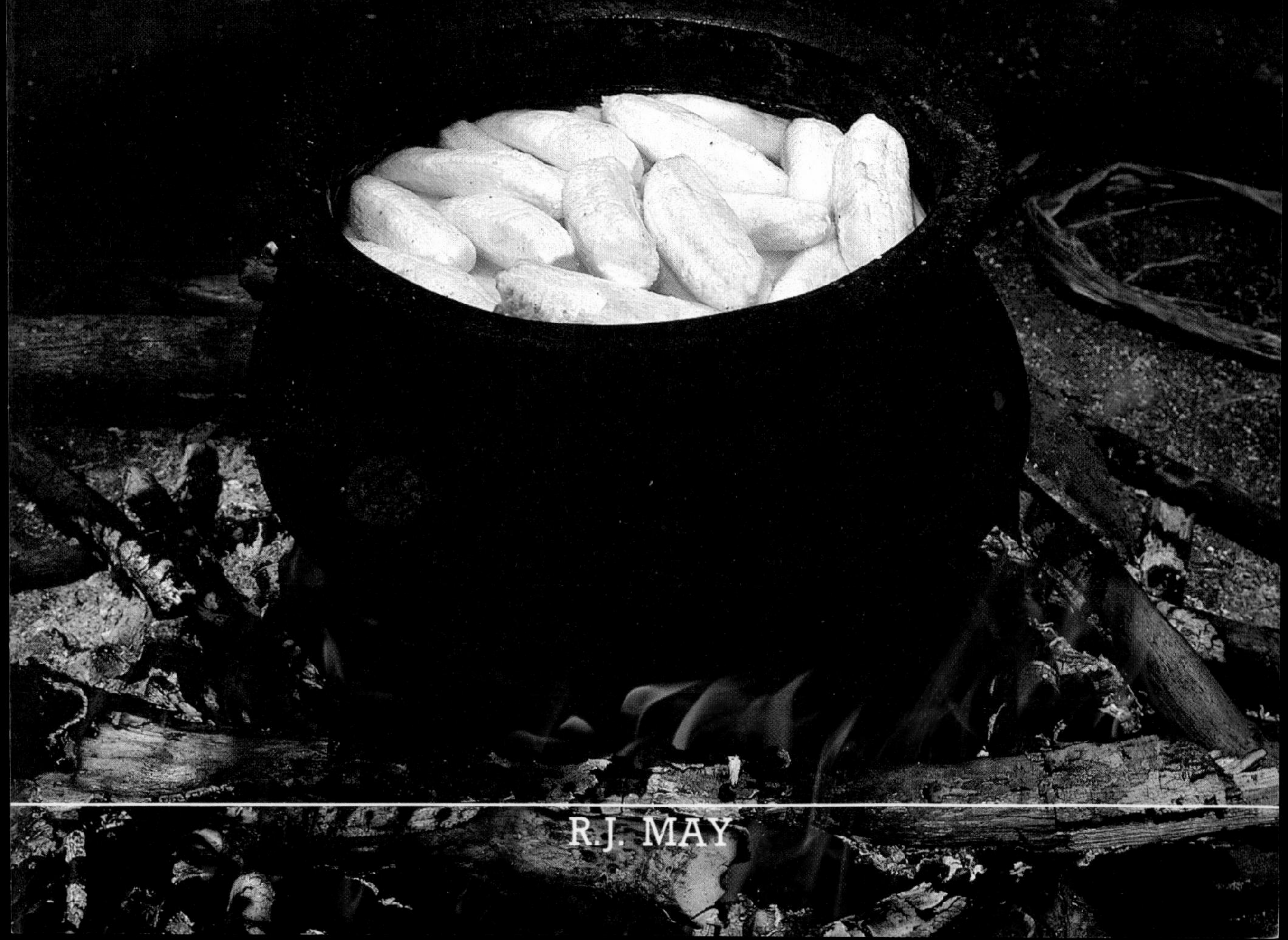

R.J. MAY

Published 1984
Robert Brown & Associates (Aust) Pty. Ltd.
P.O. Box 29,Bathurst, N.S.W. 2795 Australia

National Library of Australia Cataloguing-in-Publication entry

---

May, R.J. (Ronald James), 1939- Kaikai Aniani
A guide to bush foods,markets and culinary arts of Papua New Guinea

Bibliography
Includes index
ISBN 0 909197 52 0 1. Cookery, Papua New Guinea. I. Title
641.5995'3

Designed by M.A. MacKenzie

Typesetting in Rockwell by WestSport Productions, Bathurst, N.S.W.

Printed and bound in Singapore by Toppan Printing Company Limited

CONTENTS

1

FOREWORD

Recent evidence suggests that Papua New Guineans were among the world's first cultivators. Before Europeans came our gardens and the bush, rivers and sea provided us generally with a comfortable subsistence. Traditional cooking was perhaps usually very simple, but gardening, hunting, gathering and feasting in particular played a major part in the social and political, as well as economic, life of the community. The magnificent yam ceremonies of the Abelam people, the massive pig exchanges of the highlanders, the beautiful yam storage houses of the Trobriand Islanders and the famous *hiri* voyages are among the many examples of this.

Since European contact eating habits have changed, often substantially and not always for the better. Few expatriates have made much effort to get to know about Papua New Guinea's traditional foods and many Papua New Guineans are abandoning traditional foods in favour of imports. Last year Papua New Guinea's imports of food and live animals amounted to K139 million. One problem has been that visitors to Papua New Guinea, and indeed many Papua New Guineans, do not know the plants, animals and seafood from different parts of the country. Another is that until recently agricultural extension was directed more to cash cropping for export than to subsistence agriculture.

A Papua New Guinea cookbook, which introduced people to the various foods of the country and contained recipes which took advantage of the variety of exotic foods which are to be found, has been long overdue. *Kaikai Aniani* fills this need. Dr May, who, with his wife, is well known for his research efforts in and on behalf of Papua New Guinea, has provided us with a comprehensive account of the bush foods, markets and culinary arts of Papua New Guinea which will be valuable not only to housewives (and househusbands?) in towns and outstations throughout Papua New Guinea, but will also be useful to teachers, nutritionists and others working in rural areas.

It is time that Papua New Guinea developed its own distinctive cuisine, both for the enjoyment and benefit of its people and of visitors to our country, and also in order to reduce our present dependence on imported foods. *Kaikai Aniani* provides a good start.

Dennis Young MP
Minister for Primary Industry

Title Page
Cooking bananas,
Markham Valley, Morobe Province

1 (*previous page*)
Preparing a ceremonial pig feast,
Mendi, Southern Highlands
Province

ACKNOWLEDGEMENTS

Directly or indirectly, knowingly and unknowingly, a number of people has contributed to this book over the years. Special acknowledgement should be made to W.C. Clarke and J.S. Womersley for their advice and comments on parts of the manuscripts ; to all those who kindly provided photographs additional to my own ; to the Lae Herbarium, Bruce R. French and Celia Bridle for providing the botanical sketches ; to Maureen MacKenzie for her design ; to Jan Bretherton and Aiva Kutson for their typing, and occasionally editing, beyond the line of duty, and to my wife and small son who acted as unpaid tasters. I am also especially grateful to Tony Crawford, who revived the project when it appeared to have lapsed and who, with his wife Jenny, their house boy Andrew, and Paul and Helen Dennett, risked indigestion by trying out nearly every recipe in the book, most of which Tony photographed. My greatest debt, however, is to the countless village people who, over the years, have borne my curiosity with an amused tolerance.

PREFACE

The traditional cooking of Papua New Guinea does not seriously rival French *haute cuisine.* It does, however, offer a variety and a range of gastronomic possibilities which are seldom fully realized either by the country's thirty-odd thousand expatriates or by the growing number of urbanized Papua New Guineans, or indeed by the village people who constitute the bulk of the country's population. When my wife and I first arrived in Papua New Guinea we had great difficulty in finding anyone, national or expatriate who could identify let alone tell us how to cook any but the most common of the fruits and vegetables in the markets. The expatriate population, for the most part, seemed content to pay high prices for weary fruit and vegetables imported from Australia; I once met an expatriate who had lived on the coast of Papua for fourteen years and had never tasted a coconut. A book entitled *Entertaining in Papua New Guinea* produced by the Country Women's Association in Papua sometime around 1970 devoted seventy-seven pages to such exotic fare as cream of asparagus soup, Texas hash and butterscotch meringue, and a little over three pages to 'local dishes'. Most Papua New Guineans were equally unadventurous about foods from outside their own district. One of our earlier would-be informants, a highlander, placed all green vegetables in one of three categories: *aibika*, which describes two traditional greens (see Chapter Three); *kumu,* a general term for greens, which covered all other familiar greens, and *samting bilong nambis* - something from the coast - a residual category of greens with which he would have nothing to do. And in Rabaul, where one may, in season, purchase avocados at three for twenty toea, it is uncommon to find an avocado eating Tolai and the fruits are fed to the pigs.

Moreover in rural villages, with the spread of easy-to-grow staples such as sweet potato and tapioca, and the ready availability of such European foods as rice and tinned meat and fish, there appears to be a gradual diminishing of the range of traditional foods commonly consumed. Recent nutritional studies suggest that this narrowing of diet - especially in the consumption of traditional greens - is associated with a noticeable decline in the nutritional standards of people's diets.

Recently the situation was probably improved a little, particularly with greater interest in subsistence agriculture and traditional foods on the part of such agencies as the Department of Primary Industry and the Nutrition Section of the Department of Public Health. But it remains difficult to obtain information on the less common foods and on ways of cooking traditional foods.

The object of this book, then, is to provide a simple guide to the foods which may be found in the markets and in the bush and seashore around Papua New Guinea, with some suggestions about how to cook them. There are doubtless omissions from the list of eatables and the collection of recipes is intended merely to stimulate the appetite. But it is a start. Much of the material has been gathered first hand but I have also drawn heavily on the works of geographers, anthropologists, botanists and agricultural fieldworkers. (By way of acknowledgement, some suggestions for further reading are included at the end of the book). With regard to traditional foods, I have attempted a fairly comprehensive listing ; in the case of introduced foods I have included only those which appear to be not well known or whose culinary potentialities are not widely appreciated (thus, for example, I have included pawpaw but not included potatoes). In the recipe section I have included a few traditional recipes but most are suggestions for cooking Papua New Guinea foods in ways not traditional to Papua New Guinea.

2 (*overleaf*)
Rabaul market, East New Britain Province

PART ONE: BUSH FOODS & MARKETS

3

CHAPTER ONE

FOOD, PLACE AND PEOPLE

THE ORIGINS OF PAPUA NEW GUINEA FOODS

There is evidence of man's settlement on the mainland of Papua New Guinea about 50,000 years ago. These early settlers were probably hunter-gatherers who lived off wild game, seafood and plants - nuts, fruits, roots and leaves - which could be gathered in the bush. The stone mortars and pestles uncovered from time to time in various parts of the country and whose origins are unknown to present populations were probably used by these hunter-gatherers to break the nuts which, it has been suggested, were an important item of their diet.

About 9000 years ago, however, people in the highlands had established gardens - making them amongst the earliest known agriculturalists in the world. By around 4000 BC, under strong influence from successive migrations of people from southern Asia, agriculture seems to have largely replaced hunting and gathering as a means of sustenance. Indigenous plants which became cultivated or at least systematically exploited included sago, sugar cane and the related *pitpit*, some varieties of banana, some species of yam, breadfruit, some species of pandanus and probably several greens (including *Amaranthus* spp., *Coleus* spp., *Rungia klossii* and *Solanum nodiflorum*). But many of the important food crops, including taro, some yams, some bananas and perhaps coconut, were introduced by the new arrivals. Probably with them also came the pig and perhaps the dog and fowl. The sweet potato, which is now the main staple crop throughout most of the highlands, was probably introduced much later. Until quite recently it was generally accepted that the sweet potato, a native of South America, came to Papua New Guinea within the last 450 years from southeast Asia, where it was taken by Portuguese and Spanish voyagers. Evidence from an archaeological site at Kuk, near Mount Hagen, now suggests that it was being grown in the highlands 1200 years ago and that, therefore, it was probably introduced via Polynesia. The present widespread distribution of the sweet potato is, however, with little doubt a recent phenomenon.

Other plants which appear to have arrived in Papua New Guinea from tropical America before European settlement include corn (maize), pawpaw and probably tobacco.

In the lowlands, shifting cultivation was consistent with the regeneration of forests, and hunting and gathering continued as a significant supplement to agriculture. Above about 1500 metres, however, forest regeneration is slow ; under the impact of 'slash and burn' cultivation and hunting techniques which used fire to drive game, forest progressively gave way to grassland, and out of necessity more sophisticated systems of agriculture evolved.

Since European contact, a number of new plants has been introduced. Notable among these are tapioca, a native of tropical America which has become an important staple in some parts of the country ; and peanuts, which have provided both a garden food and a cash crop. Other successful new arrivals include the potato, carrot, onions, cabbage, Chinese cabbage and Chinese lettuce, beans, tomato, pineapple, watermelon, citrus fruits, passionfruit, custard apple, soursop and avocado.

Other notable additions to traditional food supplies include beef cattle, deer and several species of fish.

All Papua New Guinea societies have their myths of the origin of foods, which often are closely tied to stories about the foundation of the village or clan. There are many hundreds of such myths ; two of them are recounted below :

> Sami, the first man, was felling a large tree to make a canoe. His dog, Diari ran off far into the bush and came to a place called Wemkungiu. The people of this village were 'bad' or 'ugly' people, with crooked limbs. As they were all out hunting Diari climbed into a tree and waited for them to return. When the last of them came back into the village Diari leapt down onto him, bit his head off, and (one might say) headed for home. Before he got back to his master Diari buried the head in the mound of a scrub-fowl.
>
> When, shortly after, the dog returned to the mound he found that the head had sprouted into a coconut tree. He took one of the fallen nuts back to his master who, after some coaxing, opened it with a cassowary bone knife and discovered a new food. (If you look at a coconut you can still see where the eyes and mouth were.)
> *From the Wiram people of the Western Province.*
>
> Once upon a time there lived a boy whose parents died and he was alone. One day he decided to climb up a tree to get some nuts. He started climbing. When he reached the top where the nuts were he started picking them and throwing them down to the ground. While he was up there the tree grew fatter and fatter and the boy couldn't climb down. So he stayed up there and he was very, very hungry so he ate the nuts and when the nuts were finished, he ate the leaves and when the leaves were finished, he ate the small branches of the tree. When he finished eating all that, his stomach was very, very big and he was up there crying. While he was crying, a bird named Horrihombil came and took him into an empty house that contained two rooms, because she wanted to help the poor little boy. He stayed in one room and he

3 (*previous page*)
A display of coconuts, sugar cane, banana bundles and strung yams, Rigo, Central Province, c1900

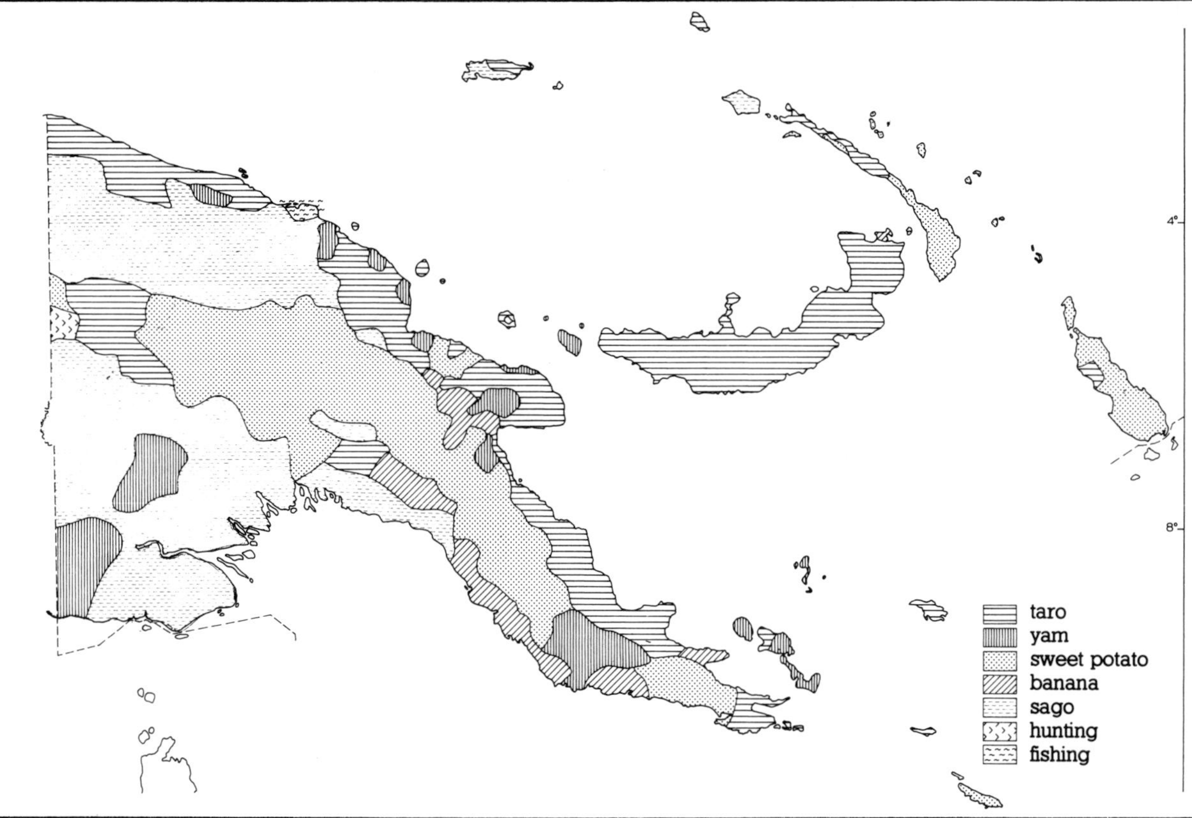

PRINCIPAL FOOD SOURCES

Source: R.G. Ward and D.A.M. Lea.
An Atlas of Papua New Guinea

passed excreta in that room and when that was filled he was moved into the other room by the bird and when the two rooms were filled, the yams began to grow. The yam spread all over the country and this is how the yam began.

From the Boiken people of East Sepik Province, as told by Maria Futo of Kumpuhun village, near Yangoru.

GARDENING AND GATHERING

Throughout Papua New Guinea the traditional diet of the people has been based on one or more staple starch foods: sweet potato, taro, yam, banana or sago. The map above shows the distribution of principal food sources throughout the country, though in most parts traditional agriculture has revolved around a combination of two or more crops. The starchy staples are usually supplemented by leafy greens and other cultivated plants, and occasionally by vegetables, fruits and nuts gathered in the bush. Pigs and, along the coast, fish and shellfish provide a major source of protein which is supplemented by other bush animals and birds and other seafood. The table below shows the composition, by weight, of daily food consumption for four villages surveyed in 1947, before imported foods became easily available.

AVERAGE DAILY FOOD CONSUMPTION FOR FOUR VILLAGES (% of total food consumption)

	BUSAMA (a coastal village near Lae)	KAIAPIT (a village in the upper Markham valley)	PATEP (a village near Mumeng Morobe Prov.)	KAVATARIA (a Trobriand Island village)
Staples and substitutes for staple	73[a]	77[b]	86[c]	85[d]
Cereals and legumes	4	1	4	-
Nuts	2	9	-	3
Green leaves	14	9	5	-
Other fruits and vegetables	7	2	4	2
Meat and fish	3	2	1	10
	100	100	100	100

[a]mostly taro
[b]mostly banana and sweet potato
[c]mostly taro and sweet potato
[d]mostly yams

(Source: Report of the New Guinea Nutrition Survey Expedition 1947, p.133)

The people of Papua New Guinea have been classified, according to their predominant agricultural practices, into three main groups: the lowlands shifting cultivators, the sago eaters, and the highlanders.

THE LOWLAND SHIFTING CULTIVATORS inhabit the forest and savannah of the lowlands, below about 1200 metres. Their main foods are taro, yam, banana and to a lesser extent tapioca. Generally in these areas, soil fertility is poor and cultivation requires long fallow periods. Garden areas are selected, sometimes fenced to keep out pigs, and are cleared by burning; this may take several weeks. Crops are then planted, often the main crop first and minor crops over a subsequent period of weeks or months. Harvesting of taro may commence within about three months of planting and yams within six or seven months, normally at the beginning of the dry season. A garden may be used for between six months and three years. A new garden site, and often a new home site, is then selected and the old garden is abandoned and allowed to revert to bush. The natural regrowth replaces some nutrients to the soil. The period of this bush fallow varies from place to place according to availability of land and other factors but is rarely less than seven years and usually more than fifteen.

The staple crops of the lowlands are supplemented by a number of cultivated plants, including coconut, breadfruit, pawpaw, mango, pandanus, betel nut, *galip* and *okari* nut and a variety of introduced fruits and vegetables. Both pigs and fish and shellfish are also important in the diet of the lowland cultivators, especially among small island communities.

4

4
Taro gardens, Wuvulu Island, Manus Province

5

5
Gathering sweet potatoes, Bilbil, Madang Province

6
Coral gardens, Misima, Milne Bay Province

7
Yam garden, near Dreikikir, East Sepik Province

6

7

8

THE SAGO EATERS mostly inhabit the extensive low-lying swampy areas of the Sepik and Fly rivers, the Purari delta and western Papua. There are, however, isolated, often semi-nomadic, sago-dependent groups in mountainous areas of the Southern Highlands Simbu, and West Sepik. Throughout a large part of this area, sago is collected from natural stands of the sago palm, but there is some selection of palms for cultivation near villages. Although sago is a popular food it is often a supplement to other staple crops and, being available all year round, is collected when other foods are scarce. The collection and preparation of sago is discussed below (pp. 52-54).

Sago is high in calories but having little protein or vitamin content, is a poor food nutritionally. Sago eaters are often able to supplement their diet with coconut, breadfruit, bananas and other plants, which can be grown on high ground in the swampy areas, and with aquatic plants, such as water lilies and the fruit of the mangrove. In parts of the Papuan Gulf, gardens are sometimes built on platforms above the water. The people of these swampy areas also obtain protein from freshwater and saltwater fish, prawns and crabs, and from game as a result of hunting. In this connection, Christian missions (such as the Seventh Day Adventists) which impose Old Testament food taboos on sago-dependent people, can have quite a deleterious effect on the protein content of an already nutritionally poor diet.

10

9

8
Washing out the sago starch, Orokolo, Gulf Province

9
Child eating sago, Aibom, East Sepik Province

10
Gogodala child eating sago, Isago, Western Province

THE HIGHLANDERS for the most part live in the intermontane valleys of the central mainland of Papua New Guinea, between about 1300 and 2300 metres, though limited gardening may extend up to another 1000 metres. Theirs is generally a more sophisticated agricultural system, with long periods of cultivation and short fallows, and often elaborate systems of drainage and mulching. Overwhelmingly the most important crop in the highlands is the sweet potato, which in places accounts for over 90 per cent of the calorific content of the diet, but in some areas it is secondary to taro, and in many parts of the highlands taro has a greater ceremonial significance.

Supplementary crops include yam, banana, tapioca, winged bean, sugar cane, *pitpit* and a variety of cultivated leafy greens; European and Chinese vegetables are also grown widely in the highlands. Pandanus, which is semi-cultivated, and other bush vegetables are collected. Pig husbandry is particularly important among highlands societies, and in the Southern Highlands cassowaries are domesticated for eventual consumption. In the less populous areas, hunting provides a significant source of protein.

As in the lowlands, gardens are prepared initially by clearing bush and burning. Once established, however, highlands gardens are typically recultivated several times before being left to fallow and the fallow period is frequently short, though practices vary widely depending on soil fertility and population density. In many parts of the highlands, drainage ditches are constructed and crops are grown in mounds built up from the loose soil; in parts of the Western Highlands compost is added to these mounds before planting. On steeply sloping land, simple terraces are often made from saplings to retain the soil.

Sweet potato may be planted at any time and in most parts of the highlands is harvested all year round though garden preparation tends to be concentrated in the latter part of the dry season. Harvesting of sweet potato takes place within about three to twelve months. Usually only a few tubers are collected at a time and an individual plant may last for several months.

With European contact there has been some diversification of subsistence gardening as well as the development of primarily export-oriented cash crops. Surprisingly, apart from passionfruit (established as a cash crop in the highlands), pineapple and perhaps custard apple and soursop, little advantage has been taken of the potential for growing such exotic fruits as jackfruit, salak, sapodilla, langsat, mangosteen or durian. Also with the spread of the cash economy, rice (a little of which is grown locally) and imported tinned fish and tinned meat have become substitutes for the traditional staple crops, and there

11
Kaukau gardens near Gumine, Simbu Province

12
Girl with cabbage, Okapa, Eastern Highlands Province

13
Kaukau gardens, Western Highlands Province

11

12

13

14 

14
Hewa arrows, Southern Highlands Province

has been a general rise in the consumption of non-traditional foods. One effect of this has been a substantial growth in the nation's outlay on imported foodstuffs - though the diversification of local food consumption is hardly sufficient to account for such bizarre occurrences as the import of coconut juice and tinned pawpaw (in one Port Moresby shop I have seen two separate brands). A second effect has been a decline in the cultivation and collection of a number of traditional subsidiary foods, which has had the common effect, according to some observers, of reducing villagers' resiliency to such adverse natural occurrences as frost and drought.

HUNTING

Except in a few remote areas, hunting is an activity subsidiary to gardening and gathering, pig raising and fishing. Nevertheless it contributes a significant source of protein to traditional diets.

Among the larger game are wild pig, wallaby, tree kangaroo, cuscus, crododile, turtle, dugong and cassowary. Other animals hunted for food include possum, bandicoot, rat, echidna, bats and a number of small marsupials. Many species of snake, lizard, frog, and insect life are collected and a wide variety of birds is used for food. Introduced game includes deer and wild cattle mostly descended from the stock of mission stations abandoned during the Second World War.

Three principal methods of hunting have been distinguished: driving, trapping and individual hunting. Driving is most commonly used in open grassland country, especially in the lowlands. Groups of hunters, often accompanied by dogs, flush game and either force it into closed areas where it can be easily killed, or drive it towards a prearranged ambush; less frequently, game is driven into nets. In many parts of the country, fire is also used to flush animals, and hunters stand on the outside of the fire killing anything which escapes the blaze. Women and children may take part in these drives, acting as beaters and adding to the noise, and often being rewarded with smaller game.

Trapping techniques consist of a wide variety of snares, box and funnel traps and pitfalls. Snares, which may be baited, are used most commonly to catch small animals and birds but they are sometimes used in hunting larger game - pig, wallaby, cassowary and crocodile. Pitfalls are most often used to catch the bigger animals.

Individual hunting usually takes the form of stalking or ambushing at feeding and resting places. Birds and bats are sometimes captured by hanging nets in cleared flight lines. In a few parts of the country, birds are also captured by covering frequently used perches with a sticky concoction made from the sap of the breadfruit tree and other trees or vines.

Dugong are hunted with harpoons from canoes, or from platforms built over known feeding grounds.

Traditionally the main weapons of the hunter are the bow and arrow and the spear, though clubs, throwing sticks, and in parts of New Britain and New Ireland, blowpipes and slings are used. A variety of arrows is used according to the purpose: broad bamboo-bladed arrows for large game (especially pigs, and in some areas previously also people), arrows with black palm, bone or hardwood heads for large and medium-sized game, arrows with several prongs for small game and birds, and blunt-headed arrows, primarily for birds with valuable skins. Since European contact, however, a good deal of hunting, especially in the coastal areas, is done with a shotgun.

FISHING

Fish form an important part of the diet of most coastal people and the people near the middle and lower courses of the larger rivers, but are rare in mountain streams. Inland streams, however, often yield eels. A wide variety of fish is eaten though some reef fish are poisonous. In recent years fresh water *tilapia*, native to Africa, have been introduced and have become an important food fish especially in inland areas.

15

15
Fishing, Goodenough Island, Milne Bay Province

16
Dugong hunters, Papuan coast, c1920
17
Fishing near Sissano, West Sepik Province, c1900
18
Fish traps, Rabaul, East New Britain Province, c1900
19
Fish traps, Rabaul, East New Britain Province, c1900

16

17

18

19

20

20
Checking fish traps, Sepik River, East Sepik Province

21
Women fishing with hand nets, Wewak, East Sepik Province

22
Communal fishing, Goodenough Island, Milne Bay Province

23
Gogodala women driving fish, Western Province

21

22

23

Fish are caught in a number of ways : with baited hooks and spinners ; with nets, traps and plunge-baskets ; with harpoons, spears, and bows and arrows ; and by drugging. Hooks and spinners are widely used in southeast Papua, along the north coast and in New Britain, New Ireland, Bougainville and Manus. Hooks are made with a variety of materials, including wood, shell, turtle shell, bone and for smaller hooks such oddities as thorns and insect legs. Hand nets and seine nets are commonly used in southeast Papua and the New Guinea islands, but net casting is uncommon. An early account of customs amongst the people of the mountains behind Yule Island, records the use of hand nets to catch small fish in mountain streams ; these nets were made by leaving cane loops standing for a few days in the bush, during which time a 'net' was constructed in the loop by orb weaving spiders. Traps and plunge baskets are widely used in coastal areas and along rivers ; these are usually woven from cane, and are occasionally lined with thorns. In a number of areas poisons are made ; a common poison is extracted from roots and stems of the *Derris* spp. These are poured into natural or man-made pools and the stupefied fish collected as they float to the surface. An alternative technique where fish or eels can be confined to small muddy pools, is to stir up the mud until the fish suffocate and float to the surface.

In New Ireland sharks are caught with a noose and float. The sharks are attracted alongside a canoe by means of a coconut rattle and bait ; when the shark is close enough, a noose, to which is attached a wooden propellor-shaped float, is slipped over its head ; the float tires the shark which is eventually dispatched with a club. Another unusual technique is practised in the Tami and Siassi islands to catch garfish and longtom. Here the fisherman uses a palm leaf kite to which is attached a cord 'baited' with a ball of spider web. The kite is flown from a canoe with the 'bait' trailing along the surface of the water ; the fish is attracted to it and becomes entangled in the spider web. Elsewhere fishermen often catch garfish at night, attracting them to their canoes by lights. But Papua New Guinea medical records reveal that the contest is not one-sided ; several fishermen have died as a result of stab wounds inflicted by leaping garfish.

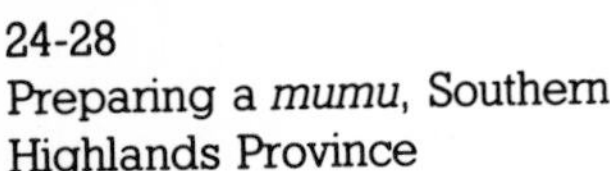

24-28
Preparing a *mumu*, Southern Highlands Province

24

COOKING AND EATING

Traditionally, food is normally cooked in one of five ways. In areas where pottery is made or traded (principally along the southeast coast, the north coast, the Markham valley, and the Madang and Sepik Provinces) food is most often boiled or steamed in pots. Frequently banana, sago or other leaves are placed on the bottom of the pot to prevent sticking, and other

26

28

29

31

30

29 31
Cooking in traditional pots, Markham Valley, Morobe Province

30
Sago grubs cooked with sago in palm leaf bundles, Western Province

32
Swamp fish cooked in bamboo, Western Province

33
Catfish stew and sago wrapped in a banana leaf bundle, Western Province

34
Roasted pig, Western Province

leaves or half coconut shells are placed on top to form a 'lid'. Very often coconut cream is squeezed into the pots as the food comes to the boil. In areas which lack pottery (and where water is often not obtained easily) food is sometimes placed, usually with a little water, into sections of green bamboo which are sealed with leaves and placed on the fire to steam. With the spread of metal cooking pots, however, this method is becoming less common. A third method of cooking, which occurs throughout the country, is the earth oven (*mumu*). An earth oven is prepared by digging a pit into which are placed hot stones, preferably evenly sized round river stones; where river stones are not easily available, pieces of coral or termites' nests are sometimes used. The food, usually wrapped in leaves (commonly banana, fig, or breadfruit), is placed in layers between the stones, with sweeter, more delicate foods on top. The whole is then covered with leaves, and sometimes earth, and left for about two hours. The process is somewhere between baking and steaming, the leaves in which foods are wrapped, supplying both moisture and flavour. Preparing an

32

33

earth oven is a time and fuel consuming task, and this method of cooking is mostly reserved for special occasions. In parts of the highlands, notably in the Simbu Province, a variation of the earth oven is made by placing hot stones, together with the wrapped food, in a hollowed section of a tree trunk. Otherwise food is usually baked or grilled, directly or in leaf or palm spathe wrapping, on an open fire. Open fires are commonly built inside houses on earthen hearths. In the middle Sepik the potters of Aibom make ornate pottery fire hearths which are used locally and traded along the river. The practice of smoking fish and meat is not uncommon. In the middle Sepik, special smoking pots, with holes, are made for this purpose, but more often meat is suspended over the fire and smoked. Some smoked meat is kept for months. An unusual practice, which occurs along the Keram River in the East Sepik Province, is the frying of sago on flat pottery dishes supported over the fire on pottery stands. Because most vegetables are either baked in their skins or cooked in water which is subsequently eaten as a soup, and because cooking time is usually short, the loss of

34

34

35

36

37

vitamins and minerals is minimized.

Most village people have their main meal in the mid or late afternoon when the day's work is finished. Leftovers may be eaten cold for breakfast but in many parts of the country, especially in the mountains where a high calorific intake is needed, people cook a small breakfast. Snacks of cold vegetables, fruit, sugar cane and sometimes small animals and insects are often eaten during the day, especially by children.

The starchy staples, which account for the greater part, by volume, of traditional diets, are generally low in both protein and vitamins. To a certain extent these needs are supplied by meat, seafood, nuts and, especially, greens (in parts of the highlands greens account for around 90 per cent of total protein intake, however, among many communities, even when these foods are fairly readily available, they are not eaten regularly, and chronic malnutrition is a problem in many parts of the country.

The composition of a number of common traditional foods is set out in the appendix at the back of this book.

TRADE

Throughout Papua New Guinea, people traditionally provide the bulk of their own food. Nevertheless food is an important component of traditional trade. In most parts of the country there is regular trade between inland and coastal people. Common exports from the inland, along with stone axes, dog teeth and *bilums,* are root crops, pandanus and tobacco; imports include sago, coconuts, smoked fish, betel nut and lime, as well as pottery and shells. The famous *hiri* trading voyages between the Motu and the people of the Papuan Gulf were based on the exchange of Motu pottery for sago. Food, especially yams and sago, play a subsidiary but fundamental part in the *kula* trade of the Milne Bay Province, and taro, sago, coconuts, pigs, fish, tobacco, betet nut and *galip* nuts are important items in the extensive trade system of the Vitiaz Straits.

For the most part, traditional trade reflects comparative advantage, usually the result of differences of physical environment. But exchanges of food fulfil social as well as economic functions.

THE SOCIOLOGY OF FOOD

Food has an importance in traditional society which goes well beyond its function of satisfying a physiological need. Indeed the anthropologist, Marie Reay has said, 'Food is esteemed because of its symbolic functions rather than because it satisfies hunger and gratifies taste. It stands for or signifies people's interests'. Magic and ceremony play an important part in gardening, hunting and fishing, and food in turn plays an important part in ceremony and in social relations generally.

Most Papua New Guinean societies have their own form of garden magic, which may include the reciting of charms or singing of songs while planting, the burying of magical

39

38

35
Hiri trading canoes, Port Moresby, c1900

36
Pots line up preparatory to *hiri* voyage, Port Moresby, c1900

37
Bundles of sago lined up for exchange, Orokolo, Gulf Province, c1923

38
Ceremonial feast, Madang Province, c1910

39
A guardian figure in a garden near Isago, Western Province

40
Yam storage houses, Kiriwina, Milne Bay Province

41
Pig exchange, Southern Highlands Province

42
Yam display, Sagisik, East Sepik Province

43
Bamboo markers indicate size of yams which have been exchanged, Nimbihu, East Sepik Province

substances in gardens, the placing of carved wooden or stone garden spirits to look after crops, and the observance of a variety of taboos, especially sex taboos, during planting and harvesting. Although some societies employ generalized garden magic, most ritual is associated with particular crops. Ethnobotanists have argued that the association of ritual with some crops rather than others may be taken as an indication of the greater traditional importance of one crop over another. In the highlands, for example, little ritual is associated with sweet potato, despite its economic predominance, though it is frequently attached to taro, which is an 'older' crop. In parts of the Sepik and Milne Bay Provinces special ceremony surrounds the planting and harvesting of yams. The Sepik yam cults generate some of the country's finest art, best known of which are the woven yam masks of the Maprik area. Although gardening is usually women's work, yam gardens are often taboo to women and it is the men who plant and harvest them, and on certain occasions cook them. There are taro cults in some parts of the country and in the Markham valley a good deal of ritual is attached to banana growing.

Magic and ritual is also employed in hunting and fishing. Most societies have charms to ensure success in pig hunting and often hunting dogs are given ginger to make them 'hot' in pursuit of game. Fishermen will seldom venture out after a big catch unless they have observed the necessary taboos and the signs are right. In 1975 a poor lobster catch at Yule Island was put down to the death of the old lady who traditionally called the westerly wind which brought the lobsters.

40

41

42

Special beliefs, seldom the same in any two communities, relate to particular foods, especially small animals. In the mid Wahgi area of the central highlands, for example, people do not eat a certain species of large fat frog because they believe that a person who ate the frog would swell up like the frog, and on Panaeate Island in Milne Bay Province, young girls do not eat flying fox meat because they believe it would make their future babies cry like the flying fox. Usually, also, people will not eat the bird or animal which is their clan totem, and most societies impose a variety of taboos on the eating of certain foods by certain people at certain times. Specific food taboos are most commonly directed at women (especially pregnant and lactating women) and children; their general effect is often to direct the best food to the older men. A more blatant form of this is the traditional practice of reserving food for the spirits; under this subterfuge, food was sent to the *haus tambaran* where it was enjoyed by the men.

Feasting and food exchanges occupy a central position in the

43

44 45

44
Short yams (*D. esculenta*) decorated as men and women, Kwamimbadu, East Sepik Province

45
Yam presentation, Bengaragum, East Sepik Province

social, economic and political life of all Papua New Guinea societies. Often feasts or *singsings* mark important events within the society: births, initiation, first menstruation, marriage, death. Sometimes, as with the nut festivals which are held in parts of the highlands, or the yam linings of the Sepik, they reflect the seasons. In the highlands the massive slaughtering of pigs for ceremonial exchange has been related to cycles in the growth of pig herds.

As well as providing the occasion for a good feed, feasts and exchanges are a means of gaining status, of renewing social solidarity and of cementing political alliances with neighbouring groups. In some parts of the country, also, competitive food exchanges are an outlet for aggression, a means of challenging and humiliating enemies. Michael Young, in describing competitive food exchanges, *abutu,* on Goodenough Island, Milne Bay, quotes his informants saying, 'Before we fought with spears, but today we fight with food'. Jim Roscoe has recorded a similar saying about food exchanges among the Boiken people of the East Sepik Province: 'Enemies fight with spears, exchange partners fight with pigs. Pigs are our spears'. In systems subject to periods of temporary surplus and recurring shortage (and bearing in mind that of all the major food crops only sago and yams can be stored for any length of time), feasting and exchange also provide a mechanism by which food may be redistributed more efficiently over time.

Usually feasts are distinguished more by the quantity of food than by its cooking, though often enough they provide the occasion for a more elaborate *mumu* than is usually the case. But some of the more interesting traditional recipes seem to be associated with ceremonial cooking. In the Maprik area a tasty thick white yam and coconut soup, *tsalingu*, is cooked at the time of yam harvesting and display, and initiation. (See recipes). A similar dish is made by Adzera men in the Morobe Province. On the Tami and Siassi islands of Morobe Province, the men prepare an interesting paste, *polom*, which is made from boiled taro, grated coconut, and coconut oil. It is mixed with a large wooden mortar and pestle and was traditionally associated with initiation ceremonies. In the Massim area a special dish of taro and certain types of cooking banana, cooked in coconut oil over a slow fire, and known on Goodenough Island as *kumakava*, appears to be reserved for special feats. The Orokaiva people of the Northern Province used to prepare a special dish, *suna*, which was given to young boys and girls at the end of their initiation and puberty seclusion, and to men who had recently slain an enemy. Ingredients varied but usually included taro, pig meat, *okari* nuts, another nut (probably *Pangium edule*), the leaves of certain trees and of croton, and sometimes breadfruit and banana. These were cooked in a combination of coconut oil and pigs' blood. Among the Adzera people of the Markham valley there is an interesting ceremonial dish, made by men and called *ganandzup*, which is made from a combination of varieties of ripe and unripe bananas cooked in coconut milk. From Wogeo Island off the Sepik coast near Wewak, Ian Hogbin has recorded a hot 'curry' made from unripe bananas and taro boiled in fresh and salt water and green coconut water, with the addition of grated raw taro, 'the peppery leaves of the *nies* plant and the pungent fruit of the *weil* plant, and, just before serving, coconut cream. Hogbin does not identify the two ingredients which obviously supply the main flavour but I have been informed that *nies* is ginger and *weil* is croton (though there is dispute as to whether croton has a pungent fruit!).

The place of food in most traditional societies is changing. Unfortunately a number of the more interesting recipes is being forgotten and many of the more marginal foods are now seldom, if ever, eaten.

46

46
Banana festival, Markham Valley, Morobe Province

47

48

49

MARKETING

In all the main centres of Papua New Guinea, and at most provincial centres and patrol posts, there are regular markets, though the variety and quality of food offered at these markets varies widely.

Justifiably most renowned is the market at Rabaul; in terms of quantity, variety and value it excels all others. There is a market every day except Sunday but it is at its best on Saturday morning. Piles of big healthy-looking taro (the main local staple) and sweet potato can always be purchased, in baskets woven from coconut leaves, as can coconut, banana and tapioca. Yam and breadfruit are sometimes available. There is usually a good variety of greens, including lettuce, Chinese cabbage and Chinese lettuce, parsley, and sometimes mint, as well as the more common traditional greens. There is almost always a wide selection of fruit, including (depending on the season) pawpaw, pineapple, guava, 'Tolai' orange, lime, mandarin, water melon, fivecorner, custard apple, soursop and passionfruit; Rabaul is the only market in which I have seen granadilla. Rabaul is also famous for its avocados. Capsicum, aubergine, tomato, beans, spring onion, choko and small sweet cucumbers are usually there. Occasionally there are other delicacies, such as turtle egg, megapode egg, and cooked fish. One seldom sees fresh fish in the Rabaul market (though they can sometimes be purchased along the north coast road). The Rabaul market also includes a number of well informed ladies who sells shells (to collect, not to eat). Strings of *tambu* shell are still used in some transactions, particularly the purchase of betel nut and lime.

Though not quite up to the standard of that in Rabaul, the main market in Lae is good. Produce from the highlands, the Markham valley and the Wau-Bulolo area supplement what is available locally. In addition to sweet potato, taro and usually some English potato the Lae market usually has a good selection of beans, cucurbits, greens and 'European' vegetables (especially tomato, capsicum, cabbage, aubergine, and spring onion). There are always plenty of passionfruit, tree tomatoes, limes and good eating bananas; usually a reasonable selection of other fruits, including banana passionfruit and *laulau*, and sometimes pandanus (*karuka*) and other nuts. There are occasionally avocados in Lae and even, I am told, strawberries. In season (around November to January) you can usually buy the long red or yellow pandanus fruit (*marita*), for around K5-K10. Sometimes there are turtle eggs and, rarely, highlands salt (see p.102). The Lae market is also a good place to buy string bags (*bilums*) and bamboo combs. It is open from

50

47
Lae market, Morobe Province

48
Roadside market near Bulolo, Morobe Province

49 50
Goroka market, Eastern Highlands Province

Monday to Saturday and is most active on Saturday morning. There is a smaller market in Lae near Butibum village.

The Goroka market is also very good, though it lacks the variety of Rabaul and Lae. It also is open six days a week and is most active on Wednesday and Saturday. The Goroka market is an excellent place to find unusual greens (and not so unusual greens, like watercress) and usually has potato and a good selection of 'European' vegetables and sometimes avocados. Pandanus is available in season and I have seen *Castanopsis* on sale there. Goroka seems to be the only market in which one sees fairly regularly the delicious tubers of the winged bean. It is also near the centre of the passionfruit industry. Mount Hagen market, which is most active on Wednesday and Saturday mornings, is not as big as that of Goroka but usually has a good selection of greens (notably *Oenanthe javanica* and *Rungia klossii*) and of European vegetables, including potato, carrot, radish, cabbage and silver beet leaves. Sometimes there are strawberries. *Bilums* may be found in the Goroka and Mount Hagen markets, usually at a fairly high price. There is a very good little market in Minj on Saturday mornings and modest markets in Kundiawa and Kainantu.

After most of these the markets in Port Moresby seem dull and expensive, but they have their compensations for those who persevere. Most of the common staples, including a wide variety of cooking bananas (plantains), are available at the various markets around Port Moresby, along with coconuts, pumpkins, cucumbers, some greens, *pitpit* and sugar cane. (In recent years Gordons market has been particularly good for greens). Breadfruit, pineapple, pawpaw, mandarin, custard apple, soursop, guava, fivecorner, lime and *laulau* are available in season. There are often bundles of sago in the main market at Koki. Both Koki and Gordon sell *tilapia* fresh and smoked and usually have fresh reef fish on Thursday and Friday afternoons; sometimes you will find live or cooked lobsters and occasionally turtle meat. Mangrove crabs and shellfish are often available as are wallaby and pork. Gordons market usually has a good range of greens, including *aibika*, amaranth, pumpkin sprouts, water *kaukau*, ferns and sometimes watercress and *Oenanthe javanica*. Polynesian chestnut, *okari* nuts and pandanus (*karuka*) may be found in Koki from time to time. The Port Moresby markets all seem to operate seven days a week but are most active on Thursday and Friday afternoons and Saturday mornings; there is also an active market at Koki on Sunday morning. The little Sunday morning market at Sogeri is quite good, especially for pineapple, eating banana (which are hard to get in Port Moresby itself), fivecorner and capsicum. Occasionally it has cooked breadfruit seeds, pandanus (*marita*) and *Castanopis* nuts.

Among the smaller markets, the town and Kreer markets in Wewak and the Maprik market are well stocked and one can often get such unusual items as flying fox, prawns, sago grubs, bamboo shoots, cooked breadfruit seeds and in Maprik 'cakes' of a cooked preparation of sago, coconut and banana or breadfruit. Angoram market is good for sago grubs, tortoise and sometimes cooked prawns. In Daru market one may occasionally find turtle and dugong meat. Alotau and Samarai markets often have unusual lowlands fruits, such as *Garcinia* and *Barringtonia*, and there is sometimes pottery from Wari Island at Alotau. Popondetta market usually has a good selection of greens and 'European' vegetables.

The fruit and vegetables on sale in the markets are generally arranged in piles or bundles costing 10t or (more frequently) 20t. Items such as pawpaw, pineapple, breadfruit and soursop and also fish, crab and meat are usually priced individually. One does not bargain.

Just about anything one finds in a market is edible though the method of cooking can be critical, (see below) but if you find something you cannot identify the sellers will usually be happy to inform you.

51
Village market, Gazelle Peninsula, East New Britain

GATHERING

In the markets one can usually find most local staples and regular items of diet and items for which there is a known expatriate demand. But there is in addition to these a huge variety of other foods, typically consumed as snacks or as famine or bush foods, which are not systematically cultivated and seldom appear in the market. In chapter three are listed all of those which I have been able to identify (with the assistance of references listed at the back under Further Reading) though I do not doubt that there are many others. Many of these are quite common (indeed several 'bush' vegetables grow wild beside the roads immediately outside Port Moresby) though often plants eaten in one part of the country are not recognized as foods in other areas where they occur. Anyone spending some time in a village is bound to meet up with at least some of these bush foods. As a general rule, however, I would advise the uninitiated to rely on local expertise in the gathering and preparation of bush foods. Many of them can be toxic if not cooked correctly and several edible plants have similar looking relatives which are poisonous.

CHAPTER THREE

A CHECKLIST OF EATABLES

The following is a list of traditional foods together with some which have been introduced. For traditional foods I have attempted to compile a comprehensive list, though there are doubtless some omissions. In each case the common English name is given first, followed in brackets by the Pidgin and then the Hiri Motu name or names (if there is no term in one of these languages I have left a blank), and finally, the botanical or zoological name. Some information is included about cooking.

ROOTS AND TUBERS

Roots and tubers provide a very large part of the traditional diet of people in most parts of Papua New Guinea. Traditionally these starchy vegetables are boiled, steamed or baked, frequently with greens or, less often, with meat; in the lowlands they are often cooked in coconut cream. Some varieties of sweet potato are good to eat raw. Yam and taro soups are made in some places, often for special ceremonies.

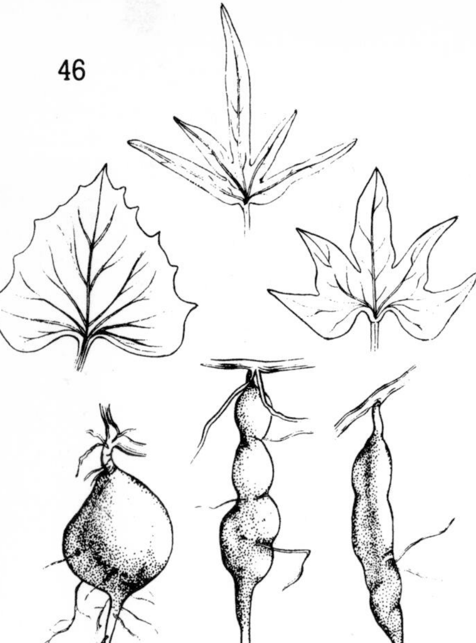

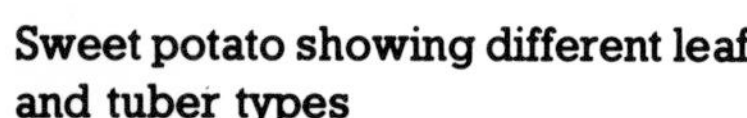

Sweet potato showing different leaf and tuber types

53

SWEET POTATO (p : *kaukau* m : *kaema*) *Ipomoea batatas*

The sweet potato is the main staple diet of most highland communities and an important item in the diet of most coastal people. It is readily available in markets throughout the country.

The sweet potato is a member of the *Convovulaceous* family. The plant, which grows along the ground, has three to five fingered, dark green leaves and a purple flower. It produces a white, cream, pink or purple coloured tuber, weighing about 50 grams to 3 kilograms. Over 350 varieties have been recorded and in parts of the highlands alone there are 65 locally named varieties. The plant grows easily from cuttings in altitudes up to 2800 metres, can be planted at any time, and is harvested within about three to twelve months of planting, depending on conditions. The young shoots may also be eaten cooked, as a green.

TARO (p : *taro ;* m : *talo*) Araceae family

In Papua New Guinea the name taro is used for several members of the *Araceae* family which have edible bulbs (corms). They are lily-like plants, usually with broad, smooth, spear or heart-shaped leaves. In the Mount Hagen area alone, thirty-one varieties of taro have been recorded.

True taro, *Colocasia esculenta,* is probably the most widespread both in gardens and occurring wild. It is a plant of about a metre or so in height. It is usually grown from a leaf-bearing section from the top of the corm and is ready for harvesting within seven to eighteen months. Another fairly common taro is *Cyrtosperma chamissonis,* or swamp taro, which is a large plant, often as high as four metres, usually found in swamps, and distinguished by its prickly stems. It produces a large bulbous corm. When cultivated, in freshwater marshes, it is seldom harvested before three years. A third member of the family, *Xanthosoma* spp., known in Pidgin as *taro kong kong,* is a relatively recent introduction. It, also, is a large plant and the flesh of its corms is coarser and has less flavour than other taros, but the plant is popular because it grows easily. It produces a large central corm, which 'fights the mouth' and is generally fed to the pigs, and a number of more palatable corms which grow off the central corm. A less common member of the *Araceae* family is *Alocasia macrorhiza,* or elephant ear taro, another large plant whose corm grows mostly above the ground. It has a high calcium oxalate content and can be toxic. *Amorphophallus campanulatus* is another wild taro which, however, lacks the characteristic spear-shaped leaves. It also has a high calcium oxalate content and is generally only used as a famine food.

Taro is probably of Asian origin (except *Xanthosoma* spp., which are native to America) but has been in Melanesia for a long time and was probably the traditional staple of a large part of the country. It occurs in damp shady places up to about 2700 metres and is widely cultivated, often on the edge of forest and sometimes in simple terraces. In the highlands taro has been largely replaced by sweet potato, but it remains the main crop in many areas, including most parts of New Britain.

Taro tubers, which vary in size from about 50 grams to 5 kilograms have a dense starchy flesh which may be white, cream, pink or purple in colour. As well as being baked, steamed or boiled, in some parts of the country boiled taro is made into a paste and in other parts a thick white soup is made. The young leaves may also be eaten. In Polynesia, *poi* is made from fermented ground taro; it is grey to mauve in colour, sour but nourishing and said to be good for the digestion.

Care must be taken in handling taro (see p.105). Some varieties, if not properly cooked, are toxic. If you do not know your taro, go for the smaller, less coarse tubers and do not peel under water.

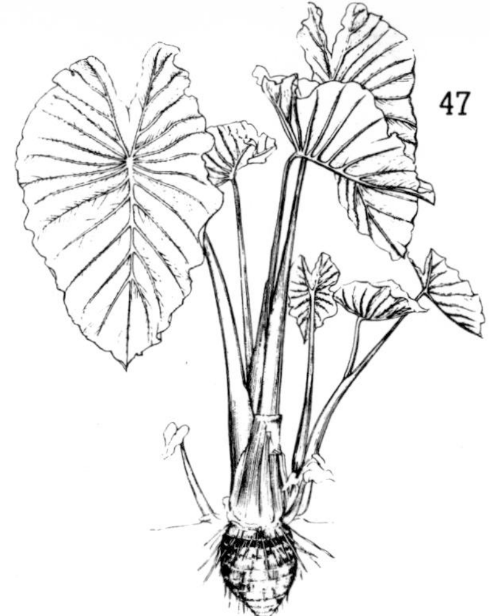

Taro tru (*Colocasia taro*)

53
Huli man eating *kaukau*, Southern Highlands Province

54
Huli women carrying *kaukau* runners, Southern Highlands Province

55
Wild taro (*C. esculenta*), Sialum, Morobe Province

56
Swamp taro, New Ireland Province

54

55

56

YAM (p : *yam, mami, patata* ; m : *maho, taitu*) *Dioscorea* spp.

Several species of yam are eaten. Some are cultivated and some are gathered in the bush, mostly in time of famine. They grow up to about 1700 metres. The two most common are the greater yam (p ; *yam* ; m ; *maho* ; *D. alata,* and the *mami* or *taitu*) (*D. esculenta*). Other common species are *D. pentaphylla*, *D. nummularia,* and *D. bulbifera.* In the Maprik district of the East Sepik Province, the heart of the yam cult area, 112 varieties of yam have been distinguished in two villages alone, bearing varietal names (such as white yam, yam like a hand, dove yam, spirit's egg yam, father yam) depending on such characteristics as the size, shape and colour of the leaf and tuber, hairiness of the tuber, colour of the shoot and taste of the yam when cooked.

The yam is a spreading or climbing vine which usually has heart-shaped leaves (*Pentaphylla* has a five fingered leaf). The root tubers vary in colour, shape and size but generally have a thin, hairy brown skin and pink, purple or white starchy flesh which is sometimes sweetish. Some species (*D. bulbifera*) also have a kidney-shaped air tuber (in Pidgin *patata*) which grows on the stem; this also may be eaten if carefully prepared (it can be toxic - see p.107). Yams are seasonal but are perhaps the only tropical tuber which can be easily stored. They may be cooked like taro and are similar in flavour. A thick white yam soup is eaten ceremonially in the Sepik.

Greater Yam
(*D. alata*)

Lesser Yam
(*D. esculenta*)

Potato Yam (*D. bulbifera*)

58
Yams on display, Trobriand Islands, Milne Bay Province

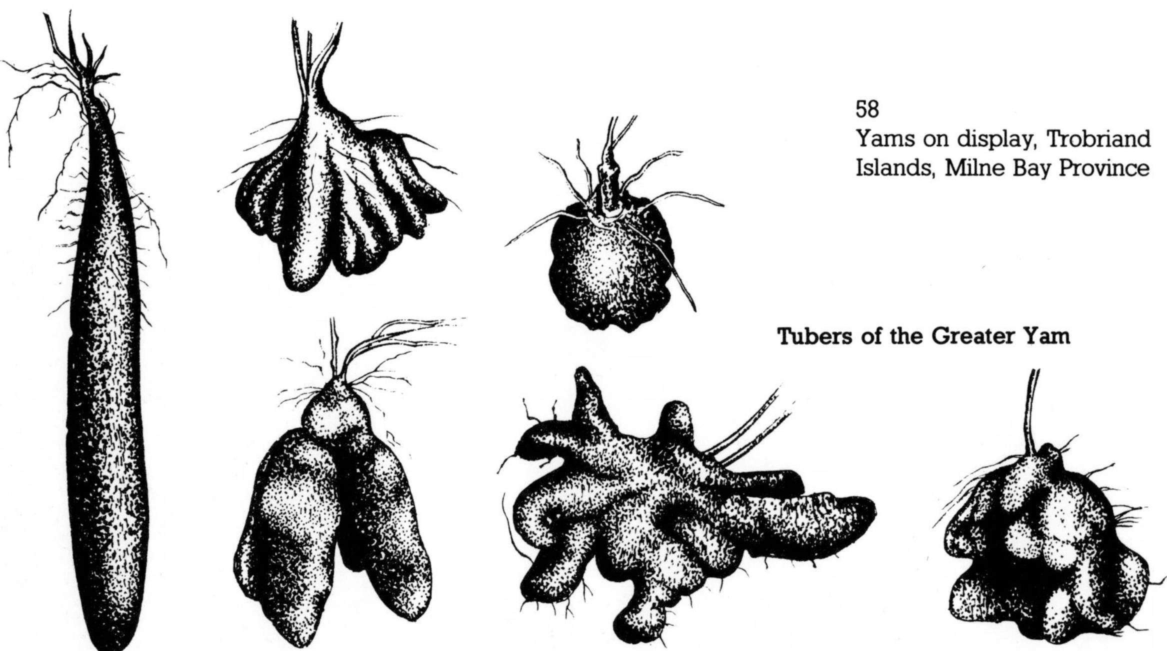

Tubers of the Greater Yam

In parts of Papua New Guinea, especially in the Maprik area, and also in the Massim area of Milne Bay Province and the Transfly of the Western Province, yams have an important ceremonial function and special yams (mostly *D. alata)* are grown for size. The tubers of these plants may reach a length of about three metres and a single tuber can weigh over 50 kilograms. In the Sepik these yams are grown in special enclosed gardens, usually on or near ridge tops. Women and uninitiated men are not allowed in the ceremonial gardens and traditionally food and sex taboos were observed by the ceremonial yam growers during the seven months or so between planting and harvesting. The planting of ceremonial yams in the Maprik area has been described by David Lea. Holes of from one to three metres are dug. A long piece of cane is placed in the middle of the hole and the earth is carefully replaced and built up into a mound of about a metre above the surface of the ground. The cane is then withdrawn leaving a small hole and the seed tuber, which has been hollowed out to prevent rotting, is placed on top of the mound with its roots over the hole ; the tuber is carefully covered with soil and the mound decorated. When the shoot is a metre long the growing point is nipped off to promote the growth of new shoots and these are trained on to cane trellises. The growing tubers are inspected every two months or so to prevent the growth of more than one tuber per plant, to loosen the soil and to administer plant magic. When the vine dies the yam is harvested ; it may take about six men to dig out a yam and carry it to the yam house where it is prepared for display and exchange. Yams may be painted and decorated with wooden or cane face masks and jewelry.

57

57
Decorated yam (*D. alata*)
Yabominu, East Sepik Province

59
Yams (*D. esculenta*)

58

59

Tapioca

TAPIOCA, CASSAVA, MANIOC

(p: *tapiok*; m: *maniota, tapioka, nao rabia*) *Manihot esculentus*

Tapioca, a native of America, was introduced into Papua New Guinea after European contact. It has since become a major staple crop in some coastal areas and in others it is an important supplementary food, especially in times of general food shortage. It is easily cultivated and grows well in poor soils but the tuber is mostly carbohydrate and has little other food value. Tapioca is a shrub, about one to three metres high, with (usually) eight-fingered leaves (resembling, I am told, marijuana). The long thin rough-skinned tubers, brown outside, white inside, may be eaten like other tubers. Alternatively the starch may be extracted by washing the grated tuber in water; this can be heated to form granulated tapioca (the form familiar to Europeans) or dried to form tapioca flour.

Several varieties of tapioca are bitter in taste and poisonous unless repeatedly washed and thoroughly cooked.

WINGED BEAN, YAM BEAN OR ASPARAGUS BEAN

(p: *hasbin*) *Psophocarpus tetragonolobus*

This versatile plant, of which there are many varieties (48 named types in the Mount Hagen area), has been a source of food, especially in the highlands and parts of the Morobe Province, for a long time. It produces long 'winged' pods whose seeds and whole young pods are eaten. The leaves and flowers are also edible and it produces small tubers about the same size as, and with similar flavour to, new potatoes. They contain about ten times as much protein per gram as sweet potato.

Queensland arrowroot plant

PUERARIA, KUDZU — *Pueraria lobata*

Pueraria is a yam-like plant with large fibrous tubers which is cultivated and also occurs wild in the highlands. It is prepared like other tubers and is said to keep well, even after cooking. Although now marginal as food, it has been suggested that this tuber may have been a much more important item of diet in the highlands before the introduction of other staple root crops. Where it is still grown it is frequently planted and harvested by men.

TURMERIC — *Curcuma* spp.

The bright orange tubers of this plant (which resembles the ginger plant) are sometimes eaten, raw or cooked. Like ginger, turmeric is usually a ceremonial food.

TANGKET, CORDYLINE

(p : *tangket*) *Cordyline terminalis/C. fruticosa*

This plant is an ancient plant well known throughout the Pacific. It is used to mark garden boundaries, is important ritually, and is worn and used decoratively. The tuber may be eaten in the same way as other tubers, but is fibrous and watery and is not a common food in Papua New Guinea. (In Hawaii the *tangket*, known as *ti*, was used to make a potent liquor, *o-kole hao*, which is now being produced commercially.)

Polynesian arrowroot plant

GINGER

(*p : kari, kawawar* ; m : *sihoa, agi*) *Zingiber* spp.

The root of ginger is eaten, raw or cooked, in many parts of the country. It is used as a flavouring but is also used medicinally and frequently plays an important part in magic.

OTHERS

Habenaria spp. is an orchid whose tubers have been reported as being used for food by the Buang people of the Morobe Province.

Queensland arrowroot *(Canna edulis)* is an introduced plant which is now grown in many coastal areas for its edible tuber. The tuber of the Polynesian arrowroot *(Tacca leontopetaloides)* is also edible, but only if carefully washed and cooked.

Water-lily *(Nymphaea* sp.) roots have been reported as an occasional food.

60
Tapioca

61
Ginger

60

61

SAGO AND OTHER STARCHES

Sago palm

SAGO (p : *saksak* ; m : *rabia*) *Metroxylon* spp.

Sago is the staple food of a large number of lowlands people and an important supplementary food for many others. It is gathered as a wild food and the palm - especially varieties without thorns - are also cultivated. Sago may be harvested all year round and unlike most tropical foods can be stored. Sago flour is high in carbohydrate but low in protein and vitamins.

Traditional methods of sago manufacture do not vary greatly from place to place. After something in the order of fifteen years a sago palm flowers, bears fruits and dies. Usually a palm is selected for sago-making just before it flowers, at which time its starch content is highest. The palm, which at this stage is around 10-15 metres high, is cut down and a section of the trunk split open to expose the fibrous white pith. This is pounded and mashed with a sago chopper. Once the pith has been thoroughly broken up it is taken to a trough (usually made from sago frond bases) where it is washed and kneaded to remove the starch. The washing trough, which is set at an incline, is open at one end and this is covered with a seive, generally made from the fibrous matting from the leaf base of a coconut or other palm. The pinky-white starchy water runs from the washing trough, through the seive, into a second trough below the washing trough, where the starch settles to the bottom. Depending on local custom the starch may be stored wet in special, large earthenware pots, collected in woven matting bags and allowed gradually to drip-dry over the fire, or dried in

62

63

64

62-68
Felling, stripping, pounding and washing sago, Isago, Western Province; the Gogodala wash their sago in a manner unlike that used elsewhere in Papua New Guinea.

67

65

66

68

69
Sago bundles drying in the sun, Misima, Milne Bay Province
70
Dry sago pancake with roasted beetle, Isago, Western Province
71
Preparing sago flour with fruit from the *tulip* tree, Balimo, Western Province
72
A 'bread' of sago, coconut and breadfruit prepared for ceremonial exchange, Maprik, East Sepik

69

the sun and stored in leaf packages. Sometimes damp sago is wrapped in leaves and buried; it ferments and may be kept for a long time. Juices of fruits *(Ficus, Citrus, Garcinia)* may be added before storage; these help break down the starch.

A single sago palm may yield around 250 kilograms of sago starch (a return of about 2.5 kilograms per man hour); in most sago eating communities this is about enough to feed one person for a year.

Traditionally there are three principal methods of cooking sago. In the first the sago flour is mixed with water - a little cold water first, then boiling water - and stirred till it thickens into a gluggy paste, at which stage it is removed from the pot (generally being twisted around a stick) and eaten ; in this form it has little flavour and is hard to digest, but is filling. A second common method is to form the moist flour into 'cakes' or 'pancakes' and cook then over an open fire. Along the Keram River in the East Sepik, sago cakes are often griddled on a flat clay dish supported over the fire on clay pot stands. Sago cakes tend to be dry and chewy, but they improve if wrapped around fish or green vegetables. Thirdly, the moist flour, sometimes with the addition of greens, may be baked in bamboo sections over a fire. As a variation on the second and third methods, in the Gulf and Western Provinces, the flour may be mixed with fruit, lotus seeds, green vegetables, sago grubs or diced meat, wrapped in palm spathe and placed over a hearth of hot embers; it is common to cook whole fish (in particular, catfish) in this manner. Sometimes leaflets are often used in lieu of palm spathe, to form a solid sago 'stick' when

70

71

cooked. Sago is also used in different parts of the country in a variety of soups. In the Sepik and elsewhere, it is mixed with coconut, banana and breadfruit and baked to form a solid 'bread'. In the highlands it may be mixed with *marita*, and either cooked as a pancake with greens or wrapped in leaves and cooked in an earth oven.

Young sago palms are occasionally cut down and the celery-like heart or bud, eaten raw or cooked. Sago grubs are also collected from felled palms (see below). In addition, sago leaves are used for thatching and matting, leaf stems are used in housebuilding, seeds are used to make jewelry, and the thorns are used as arrow heads.

CYCAD (p: *baibai*) *Cycas circinalis*

Cycas circinalis is a small palm-like plant common around Port Moresby. It has a pithy centre from which starch can be extracted (starch is also extracted from the seeds see p. 81) but it must be thoroughly washed as the plant is otherwise poisonous. The cycad is eaten in various parts of the country but appears to be used only as a last resort famine food.

Starch can also be extracted from the pithy centre of a species of *Caryota* palm.

73
Mixing sago jelly, Sowanda, West Sepik Province

74
Cycas circinalis

73

72

74

GREEN LEAVES AND SHOOTS

75 

75
Buying *aibika*, Gordons market, Port Moresby, National Capital District

76
Aibika

77
Amaranth

A variety of leafy greens is eaten throughout the country. Greens are an important source of protein and minerals in traditional diets. Some are cultivated in gardens, but many are bush vegetables which are not regularly eaten, except in times of general food shortage. Traditionally, greens are usually cooked with meat and vegetables to add flavour and moisture; only occasionally are they eaten by themselves. Most, however, can be eaten as 'spinach'. Cook lightly with a minimum of salted water, and for additional flavour add a little butter and lime juice. It is advisable to strip the leaves from the stems before cooking.

The practice of eating greens varies widely from place to place and it is not uncommon to find that a green which is eaten in one area is not recognized as a food in another. For the same reason it is difficult to collect data about greens; although different varieties usually have different names in the local language there is little differentiation in Pidgin (the term *kumu* is used for greens generally), and it is not always easy when in the field to carry back samples for botanical identification. The following is a list of greens found in markets around the country together with some which have been recorded by field workers.

AIBIKA (p : *aibika*) *Hibiscus manihot Abelmoschus manihot*

This is one of two common traditional green vegetables called *aibika* in Pidgin. Its five-fingered leaf grows on a thick green or red stem, on a bush or small tree. It is a very glutinous (some say slimy) vegetable, and as such not very pleasant on its own. However, it lends moisture to vegetables cooked in an earth oven, and is a good soup vegetable. Chapter 6 gives a recipe for a soup (mock melokhia) which happily combines this and the other common *aibika*.

Amaranthus

AMARANTH (p : *aibika, aupa*) *Amaranthus* spp.

This is the other green referred to in Pidgin as *aibika* (or as *aupa*). It is a small plant which grows profusely. The leaves may be dark green or combinations of green, yellow and red. Usually the whole plant is pulled out when it is about 25 centimetres high, before it goes to seed. For cooking, it is best to take the leaves off with a minimum of stem, and lightly steam. It has a flavour and texture something like European spinach, though less moist, and is good as a green on its own or in soup. It is found in markets all over the country and is easily grown. It

76

77

78

78
Water *kaukau*

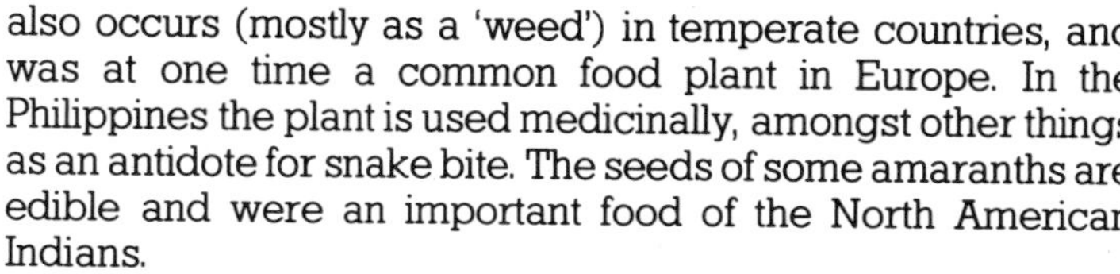

also occurs (mostly as a 'weed') in temperate countries, and was at one time a common food plant in Europe. In the Philippines the plant is used medicinally, amongst other things as an antidote for snake bite. The seeds of some amaranths are edible and were an important food of the North American Indians.

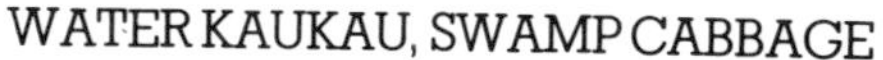

WATER KAUKAU, SWAMP CABBAGE
(p : *kangkung*) Ipomoea aquatica

This is an aquatic plant which has hollow stems and usually spear-shaped leaves. It is related to the sweet potato but has no tubers. It grows wild in swampy places (including several swampy areas of Port Moresby) but is also cultivated; its leaves provide one of the principal greens of people along the Sepik River. The leaves have a somewhat sharp taste and are a little glutinous, but are pleasant when steamed. They may be mildly laxative.

Water *kaukau*

79 *Tulip* **tree**
Pumpkin tips

80
Tapioca leaves

81
Coral tree leaves

82
Ferns (*Cyclosorus* sp.)

79

TWO-LEAF, JOINTFIR SPINACH
(p : *tulip;* m : *kemu*) *Gnetum gnemon*

The shiny young leaves of this tree (the leaves grow in pairs — hence the name, 'two leaf') are a popular food in both coastal and highlands areas. They have a strong, somewhat meaty taste and tend to be firm and chewy. They are excellent when cooked with meat or vegetables or steamed on their own. The young inflorescences of this tree can also be eaten as can the olive-shaped fruit (see below), and the inner bark of the tree is used for making tapa cloth and string.

PUMPKIN AND OTHER CUCURBIT SPROUTS
(p : *lip pamken ;* m : *mausini rauna*) *Cucurbita pepo* etc

The shoots, tendrils and young leaves of the pumpkin vine are widely used as a green. They have a good mild flavour but tend to taste furry and have a stringy texture. Pumpkin shoots should be lightly steamed; too much moisture and they are soggy. They are excellent for making soups, especially if a strainer is used.

The young shoots of the gourd, the choko, the squash and several other cucurbits are similarly edible.

TARO LEAVES (p : *lip taro ;* m : *talo rauna*) *Araceae* family

Taro leaves (principally *Colocasia esculenta)* are frequently used as a green, especially with foods cooked in earth ovens. Boiled, the leaves tend to be slimy. The same caution should be observed in the preparation of taro leaves as in the preparation of the tubers (see above).

KAUKAU LEAVES
(p : *lip kaukau ;* m : *kaema rauna*) *Ipomoea batatas*

Young *kaukau* leaves are often eaten in the highlands, though mostly as a scarcity food. They are usually steamed with meat or root vegetables and have a slightly bitter taste.

PAWPAW LEAVES
(p : *lip popo ;* m : *loko rauna*) *Carica papaya*

The young leaves of the pawpaw may be eaten if cooked carefully, changing the water at least twice.

80

TAPIOCA LEAVES

(p : *lip tapiok ;* m : *maniota rauna*) *Manihot esculentus*

The young leaves of the tapioca plant may be eaten, if well cooked. Like *kaukau* leaves they tend to be bitter and are usually regarded as a scarcity food, though they are very nutritious.

BEAN LEAVES

(p : *lip bin ;* m : *bini rauna*) Various

The cooked leaves (and the dark blue flowers) of the *hasbin* are a popular green, especially in the highlands. They have a slightly sweet flavour. The leaves of the hyacinth bean and the lima bean - and probably others - are also edible.

81

WILD FIG LEAVES

(p : *kumu mosang) Ficus* spp.

The young leaves (and the fruit) of several species of wild and semi-cultivated fig are eaten, especially in the highlands where they are often used as a lining or wrapping in earth ovens. Most fig leaves, even when young, are large and coarse, and unless very well cooked taste rather like unbleached calico. The following species of *Ficus* have been recorded as having edible leaves : *F. copiosa, F. cynaroides, F. dammaropsis, F. iodotricha, F. nodosa, F. pachyrachis, F. pungens, F. robusta, and F. wassa. Ficus* trees also supply bark which is used to make cloth and string.

82

CORAL TREE

(p : *balbal*) *Erythrina variegata*

The yellow and green pungent leaves of this tree (which is a common ornamental tree in Papua New Guinea towns) are eaten in some places, notably along the Sepik River where I have been told that they were traditionally used in the cooking of human skulls. The tree is also associated traditionally with cannibalism in parts of the Madang Province. The leaves are probably best used sparingly as a flavouring.

FERNS

Various

A number of ferns, terrestrial and parasitic, are used in traditional cooking. A number, also, are poisonous however, and it is therefore unwise to eat ferns unless one is sure of the edibility of the plant and the method of cooking.

A terrestrial fern often on sale in the markets in Port Moresby,

Rungia

83
Oenanthe javanica and *Rungia klossii* growing in a garden near Minj, Western Highlands Province

83

Lae and Rabaul is a species of *Cyclosorus.* It has pale green fronds about 40cm long which may be cooked like other greens; they have a fresh, slightly sweet taste. Other genera of ferns occurring in Papua New Guinea which are recorded as being edible are *Alsophila* (a tree fern); *Asplenium; Athyrium* (fishnet fern : Pidgin *perepere*); *Ctenitis; Cyathea* (a tree fern whose young leaves, cooked, are a common food in parts of the highlands); *Dennstaedtia; Diplazium; Dryopteris; Lycopodium; Polypodium; Pteridophyta* and *Stenochlaena.*

CASSIA *Cassia* sp. (*?C. leschenaultiana*)

The pinnate leaves of this tree provide a fairly common lowlands green, which is often available in Port Moresby. It makes a pleasant vegetable.

'BLACK NIGHTSHADE' (p : *karakap*) *Solanum nodiflorum*

The 'black nightshade' (not to be confused with 'deadly nightshade', *Atropa belladonna*) which is used as a food plant in Papua New Guinea was, until recently, generally described as Solanum nigrum, but is now recognized as a separate species. It belongs to the same family as the potato. In Papua New Guinea, *Solanum nodiflorum* has long been cultivated for its edible leaves and several observers have recorded that the black berries are also eaten (see p.79). The leaves are soft in texture and have a rather bitter taste. 'Nightshade' does not appear to be a common food (though we have a selfsown plant in what goes for our garden) and is unlikely to be encountered in the market.

WATER DROPWORT *Oenanthe javanica*

This is a small green herb (in the Medlpa language, *kun,* and in the Middle Wahgi language, *kunjigl*) with pale green leaves rather like parsley, which grows in small clumps close to the ground. It is used extensively in the highlands as a cooked green, and is also used in magic. It is pleasant as a salad vegetable, having a fresh, slightly bitter taste, rather like fennel. It is common in highlands markets and recently has appeared in Port Moresby. I have stripped the leaves of a bunch bought at Gordons market and had two more 'crops' by letting the stalks stand in a jug of water; they root easily.

RUNGIA *Rungia klossii*

Rungia is a small plant with dark green and yellow leaves and blue flowers, which grows in clumps about 30 centimetres high and is used primarily as a flavouring in highlands cooking. It is cultivated and also occurs wild. The leaves may be eaten cooked or in salads (raw, they have a rather sharp flavour). I have seen the plant (in the Medlpa language, *kenkaba* and in the Middle Wahgi language, *aimbe*) in the Mount Hagen and Minj markets.

Highland *pitpit*

COMMELINA, WANDERING JEW *Commelina* spp.

This is a group of small trailing plants cultivated and gathered in the wild in the highlands. The leaves may be cooked (they are a popular green with pork) or eaten raw, sometimes with salt.

WATER CRESS (p : *kango*) *Nasturtium officinale*

Watercress is a recently introduced plant but is common where there is water, and is frequently available in markets around the country. It is good to eat as a salad vegetable but may be cooked and makes an excellent soup (see recipes).

CRESS, LEAF MUSTARD (p : *kares, kari*) *Rorippa* spp.

This is a genus of small plants with pale green leaves and tiny yellow flowers, which may be found in highlands markets and appear occasionally elsewhere. They have a sharp, mildly bitter taste and may be eaten as a salad green or cooked.

84
Watercress

84

WILD MULBERRY LEAVES
(p : *burua*) *Broussonetia papyrifera*

The dark green oval leaves of this tree are sometimes cooked and eaten. The inner bark of the tree is used to make tapa cloth.

PIGWEED, PURSLANE, PORTULACA *Portulaca oleracea*

Pigweed is a creeping, succulent plant with fleshy leaves and yellow flowers, especially common along sandy coastlines (not to be confused with the giant pigweed, *Triathema portulacastrum*, which has pink flowers and is reported to be poisonous). Although it does not appear to be widely eaten in Papua New Guinea, it is a familiar food in other parts of the Pacific, and was one of the greens used by Captain Cook to combat scurvy. All parts of the plant may be eaten raw or cooked. The Australian aborigines also prize the small black seeds.

85
Pitpit; Saccharum edule (left) and *Setaria palmifolia* (right)

86
Bamboo shoots

85

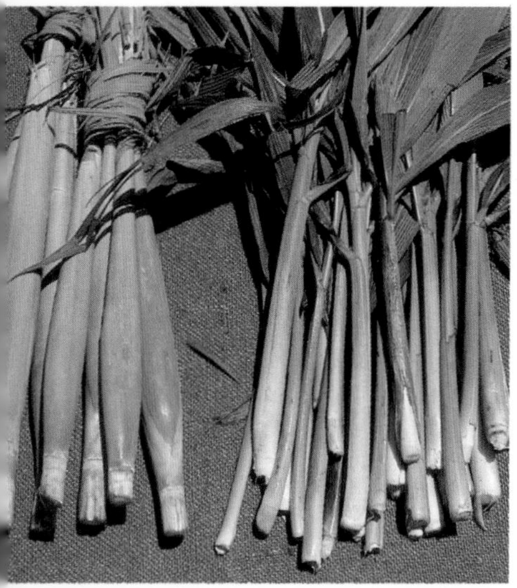

86

NEW GUINEA ASPARAGUS, HIGHLAND PITPIT
(p : *pitpit*) *Setaria palmifolia*

This is a coarse grass which is cultivated and occurs wild. Cultivated varieties are found in most markets around the country. Many varieties exist, some with broad, dark green leaves, some with red. The soft inner shoot of the plant is eaten, and in the market the bundles of these long thin greens may be mistaken for the enclosed inflorescences of *Saccharum edule* (also called *pitpit*). (See p.82).

Strip the outside leaves and steam or bake. The cooked vegetable tastes something like corn-flavoured asparagus. The soft inner shoot may also be eaten raw.

PALM HEARTS Various

The centre shoots or hearts, sometimes called the 'cabbage' (in Pidgin, *kru*) of several species of palm may be eaten cooked or raw. Consumption of the heart, of course, kills the tree. Among those recorded as being eaten in Papua New Guinea are the hearts of the coconut palm (in other countries this is sometimes referred to as 'millionaire's salad'); the sago palm; *Gronophyllum chaunostachys* (a tall mountain palm) ; and species of *Archontophoenix, Arenga* (the sugar palm, a thin palm which also yields a sweet sap) and *Caryota*. The soft base of the developing fruits of *Nypa fruticans* is similarly eaten. The flavour of palm hearts is often compared to that of celery, though coconut heart has a somewhat nutty flavour.

BAMBOO SHOOTS (p : *kru mambu;* m : *bau*) *Bambusa* spp.

In some parts of Papua New Guinea, the young shoots of several species of bamboo are eaten, cooked or raw. The taste is much the same as the tinned commodity imported in substantial quantities from China!

OTHER GREENS

The above list covers most of the greens (other than common European vegetables) and shoots which are likely to be encountered in markets around the country, and some which one is not likely to encounter. Numerous other greens are eaten in different parts of the country, especially as famine foods and during expeditions in the bush. The following is a supplementary list, taken mostly from William Clarke's *Place and People* and Straatmans's ethnobotanical checklist.

Acalypha sp.	a tree with edible red leaves, which are sometimes chewed and spat on pork at ceremonial feasts.
Albizia sp. (*?A. procera*) (p : *pounpoun;* m : *bikeke*)	a tree whose young leaves are eaten. (The bark and fruit of some species of *Albizia* however contain saponins).
Astronia sp.	a small tree with edible leaves.
Begonia	the leaves and stems of wild begonias are eaten in the highlands.
Celosia argentea	quail grass, a member of the amaranth family.
Centella asiatica	a creeping herb with edible leaves.
Chemopodium sp.	shrub with edible leaves.
Chloranthus officinalis	a woody herb whose leaves are eaten.
Cinnamomum sp.	wild cinnamon; the leaves are eaten.
Coleus scuttellarioides	a herb eaten with salt. (Seeds of a *Coleus* sp. found at an archaeological site near Mount Hagen suggest that this may have been, historically, a regular item of diet in the highlands.) Other species of *Coleus* are edible.
Deeringia amaranthoides	a member of the amaranth family with pinkish green leaves (and bright pink berries which are not eaten).
Desmodium microphyllum	a large herb with edible leaves.
Enhalus spp.	a sea grass, is eaten, boiled, in some places.
Euodia spp.	(Motu, *ebala*) a tree whose lemon-scented leaves are occasionally used, fresh or dried, as a flavouring.
Freycinetia montana	a climbing plant, related to the pandanus, whose young leaves are eaten.
Graphtophyllum pictum	a herb whose green and red leaves are eaten in the highlands.
Impatiens sp.	a herb with edible leaves.
Intsia bijuga (p : *kwila;* m : *manea*)	a coastal tree with edible leaves.
Kleinhovia hospita	a forest tree whose heart-shaped leaves are eaten cooked.
Medusanthera papuana	tree with edible leaves.
Miscanthus japonicus	a grass whose young shoots may be eaten.
Morinda citrifolia	the young leaves of this tree may be eaten and are sometimes used as wrapping in earth ovens (also see p.78).
Moringa oleifera	the horseradish tree, probably a fairly recent arrival; young leaves eaten.
Phrynium sp.	leaves used to line earth ovens and young unfurled leaves eaten raw.
Pilea sp.	a small herb apparently used as flavouring.
Pipturus argenteus	a small shrub whose leaves are eaten.
Polyscias spp.	a leafy bush whose young leaves are edible; in parts of the highlands the leaves are chewed with salt and then spat onto meat and pandanus; the plant is also common in East New Britain, where its *kuanua* name is *valingur*.
Pouzolzia hirta	stem and leaves eaten after cooking in earth oven.
Saccharum spontaneum	a shoot like *pitpit*.
Sesbania grandiflora	a small tree whose young leaves may be eaten.
Sterculia bamleri	a forest tree with edible leaves.
Tephrosia sp.	the leaves of an unidentified species of this shrub are reported to be eaten. In other countries, however, species of *Tephrosia* are used variously as a fish poison, arrow poison, abortifacient and cure for mange.
Zingiber spp.	the young leaves of the cultivated ginger plant have been recorded as a cooked green.

CUCURBITS, LEGUMES AND OTHER VEGETABLES

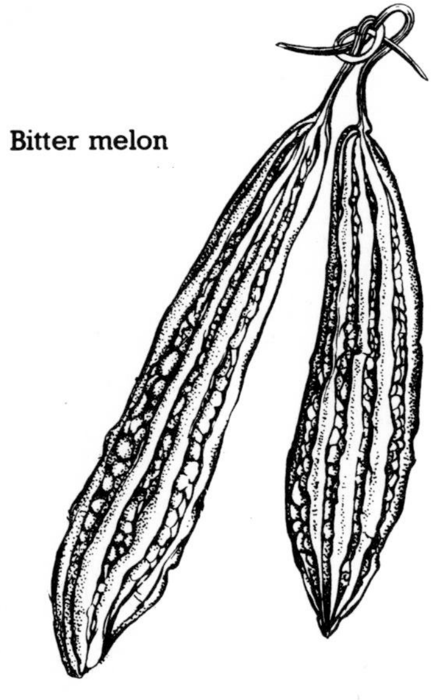
Bitter melon

Several cucurbits, cultivated or semi-wild, traditionally supplemented the main staples; a number of new varieties have been introduced since European contact. In most cases these climbing plants are eaten both as a vegetable and as a green.

PUMPKIN (p : *pamken :* m : *mausini*) *Cucurbita pepo*

The pumpkin appears to be a traditional vegetable found in most parts of the country. In markets one often sees a long green and yellow-skinned variety and a small, sweet, grey-brown (butter nut) pumpkin. Pumpkin can be cooked in several ways but is perhaps best baked with lots of butter. The cooked seeds are sometimes eaten as a snack.

GOURD (p : *kambang :* m : *popou*) *Lagenaria siceraria ; Trichosanthes* spp.

The gourd is believed to be an ancient vegetable in Papua New Guinea and to have once been more important as a food than it now is. The young fruits of *Lagenaria* are juicy and sweet when cooked and the shoots provide a tasty green. The dried outer shell of old fruit is commonly used as a container for water, lime, salt, oils or grease. The fruit of *Trichosanthes* (which includes the snake gourd) should also be eaten when young; in older fruit the flesh is red and bitter (due to glucosides) and it seems that only the seeds are eaten.

CUCUMBER (p : *kukamba ;* m : *kuikamba*) *Cucumis sativus*

The cucumber is another traditional vegetable. The local variety is usually yellow or brown and is larger and usually drier than the dark green variety familiar to Europeans (and now common in the highlands).

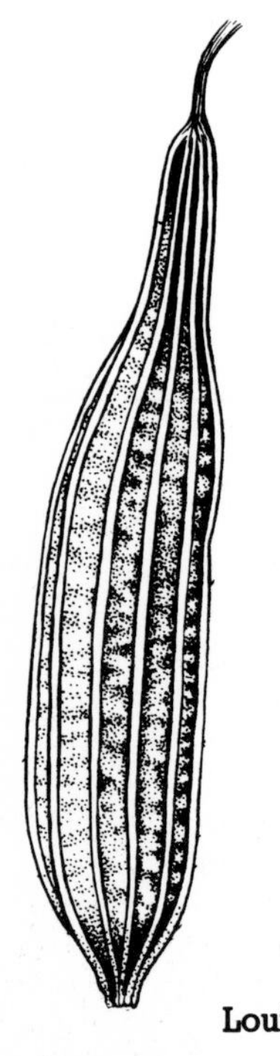
Loufah

BITTER MELON, BALSAM PEAR *Momordica charantia*

Another cucurbit, less familiar to Europeans than Chinese, is the bitter melon. In its best-known cultivated form, which has been recently introduced, this plant produces a green wrinkled fruit about 10 to 15 centimetres long. The fruit should be eaten boiled or steamed when it is young; as it gets older the fruit becomes very bitter. A wild variety, found along the roadsides around Port Moresby, produces a smaller orange fruit with a warty surface which contains a bright red edible pulp and black seeds.

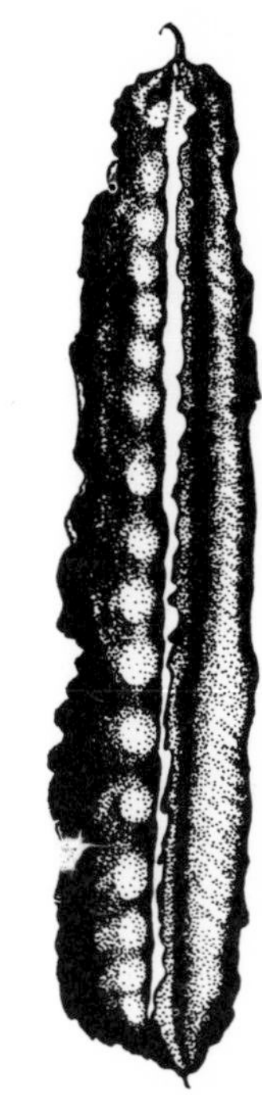

Winged bean

CHOKO, CUSTARD MARROW (p : *sako*) *Sechium edule*

The choko is probably a recent introduction though some people claim that it predates European settlement. The plant produces a pear-shaped, ribbed, green fruit with soft spines. The fruit may be eaten cooked or raw (cooked, it tastes vaguely like squash).

OTHER CUCURBITS Various

In highlands markets I have bought an unidentified traditional cucurbit which looks like a cross between a yellow skinned cucumber and a pawpaw. In the Middle Wahgi language it is called *gol mung.* The fruit has a yellow flesh, which, when cooked, tastes like a rather insipid pumpkin, and a large number of black seeds surrounded by a bright red pulp. The ripe fruit is usually full of small white grubs; eat them - they give the fruit a nutty taste.

Loufah (*Luffa* spp.), which I have come across in the Markham valley, are longish green vegetables with a ridged skin. Like gourds they should be eaten young; they tend to become dry and bitter.

87

87
Pumpkins

88

88
Gol mung

89

90

Other edible cucurbits apparently not recently introduced include *Citrullus vulgaris*, the watermelon; *Cucumis melo*, the Pacific melon, and *Melothria* spp. (commonly known in Southeast Asia as 'mouse gourd' or 'mouse cucumber'). In China, dried watermelon seeds are eaten like peanuts.

BEANS (p : *bin* ; m : *bini*) Various

The seeds, pods, leaves, and in at least one case (the *hasbin*) the roots, of several beans and peas provide food.

Probably the most widespread of these is the winged bean or *hasbin (Psophocarpus tetragonolobus)*, already described as a tuber and a green. All parts of this traditional food plant may be eaten. The 'winged' pods are green or deep reddish brown and grow up to about 25cm. The whole young pods can be eaten or the red seeds extracted from the mature pod and eaten raw or cooked.

Another traditional bean is the hyacinth bean (*Lablab niger/L. purpureus/Dolichos lablab*), the leaves, young pods and seeds of which are eaten. This bean occurs semi-wild and is sometimes cultivated. A third bean which appears to be long established is the lima bean (*Phaseolus lunatus*) whose seeds, pods and leaves are eaten. Noncultivated varieties of both the hyacinth bean and the lima bean should be treated with caution: if bought in a market they are probably safe but wild varieties may be toxic; wild lima beans (specifically those with dark seeds) have been known to cause death. The yard long bean (*Vigna sesquipedalis*) also appears to be a traditional food, the pods and seeds being eaten.

In the Minj area there is a flat bean known locally as the 'spirit bean' (*kipe bar*). It is said that this bean is not poisonous but that if a person eats it and then goes to a river where there are spirits, the spirits will smell *kipe bar* on the person's breath and will enter the stomach in search of food; this will make the person ill and he or she could die.

Other, more recent, introductions include the common or snake bean (*Phaseolus vulgaris*), mung bean (*Vigna radiata* or *Phaseolus aureus*), pigeon pea (*Cajanus cajan*), long bean or cow pea (*Vigna sinensis*) and jack bean (*Canavalia ensiformis*). In most cases pods, seeds and leaves may be eaten.

PEANUT (p : *pinat, kasang* ; m : *pinati*) *Arachis hypogaea*

The peanut is a recent introduction but is now an important item of diet in most parts of the country. Although peanuts are good to eat raw, they have little nutritional value unless cooked or mashed. Peanut butter is now manufactured in the Morobe Province.

89
Winged beans

90
Peanuts

NUTS AND FRUITS

Nuts, particularly coconut and pandanus, are an important item of diet in Papua New Guinea, and there is a good deal of archaeological evidence to suggest that, historically, they were much more important than they are now.

Apart from banana, breadfruit and to a much lesser extent some wild figs and mangrove fruit - which except for some bananas are eaten as vegetables - fruits are relatively unimportant in traditional diets. Given the favourable climate, it is remarkable that attempts to introduce exotic tropical fruits, particularly from southeast Asia, have met with such little success. Nevertheless, there is a number of fruits, indigenous or introduced, to be found around Papua New Guinea, many of which may not be well known. The following list contains traditional fruits and some lesser known recent introductions.

91
Man drinking coconut milk, Collingwood Bay, Northern Province c1911

COCONUT (p: *kulau, kokonas;* m: *karu, niu*) *Cocas nucifera*

The coconut palm is an indispensable element in the economies of tropical islands and wet lowland communities throughout the world. The tree supplies wood for building (if better alternatives are not available); the leaves are used in matting and thatching; the fruit supplies food and drink, and in more recent times an opportunity for cash income; the used nut and dry leaves supply fuel; cups and spoons may be made from the hard wood of the nut, and the heart of the palm may be eaten. In some parts of the world coconut oil is burnt for light, and toddy, a sweet juice which ferments rapidly, is made from the sap. It is generally believed that the coconut was carried to Papua New Guinea from southeast Asia centuries ago; recent evidence, however, suggests that it may be indigenous to the Pacific. It is an important source of food to large numbers of lowland and island people.

Most coconut palms take about eight years to produce fruit but a palm may go on bearing for over a hundred years. Under plantation conditions a single palm may yield over sixty nuts per year. A nut takes about twelve months to mature. As it matures the husk changes in colour from green to yellow; husked, green coconuts can easily be distinguished from older nuts by their paler shell.

The water from green coconuts (p: *kulau;* m: *karu*) is deliciously refreshing, especially if the whole coconut can be chilled; slice the top off and drink straight from the nut (or from a straw if you dribble). A nut usually contains the maximum liquid at

92

about four months and a good nut may contain around a litre. The soft flesh, or jelly, of green coconuts can be eaten off the shell and the husk of young coconuts may be chewed like sugarcane. As the nut gets older the liquid is absorbed into the flesh of the nut ; the flesh gets harder and thicker. At this stage the flesh (or 'meat') provides a nourishing meal raw or roasted in the shell. If you get a coconut which has begun to shoot (they are usually available at Koki market) you can eat the round 'embryo', sometimes called the 'apple' or 'bread' (actually a transferred endosperm prior to germination), which forms inside the nut ; it is fluffy and sweet. The young shoot may also be eaten like celery. Coconut milk is an essential ingredient for cooking (see Chapter 5).

PANDANUS (p : *karuka, marita* ; m : *geregere*) *Pandanus* spp.

The pandanus are a family of trees which occur widely throughout the country, from small coral islands to high mountains. The fruits of a number of species are eaten; pandanus leaves are also used in matting and thatching. In the highlands, pandanus is often referred to as *Kokonas bilong mipela.* Pandanus trees are sometimes cultivated but the fruit, which is seasonal, is also gathered from wild and semi-wild trees. Disputes over rights to pandanus trees have long been a major source of friction among highlands people, by whom the fruit is highly prized.

The fruit (syncarp) of the pandanus is eaten in three principal forms. Several species produce a round brown composite fruit superficially similar in appearance to a pineapple, and

93

94

frequently about the same size, which consists of a large number of finger-sized segments or phalanges. The kernels of these segments are white and oily and taste a little like coconut. They may be roasted or eaten raw. In the highlands they are often smoked and kept for several months. In this form, pandanus is referred to in Pidgin as *karuka.* The principal species seem to be *P. julianeti* and *P. brosimos.*

In some other species, especially those near the coast (in Motu, *geregere*), each segment of the fruit is covered with a soft, sweet, orange-yellow pulp which, when ripe may be chewed or scraped into water to make a sweet drink. This pulp, however, is often highly astringent and may 'fight the mouth'; roasting the fruit first or boiling the liquid lessens this. In some parts of the Pacific, pandanus (notably *P. Pulposus*) is grown specifically for the pulpy fruit, from which a paste and flour is also made.

In its third main form pandanus is known in Pidgin as *marita.* The *marita* is a lowland to middle altitude species (*P. conoideus*), which is cultivated, semi-cultivated and occasionally gathered wild. It produces a long red or yellow fruit which may be more than a metre long and weigh up to 10 kilograms. It consists of a large number of small segments on a central core. Methods of preparation of *marita* vary but a common procedure is to cut the fruit into sections (the size of the sections depending on the method of cooking) and boil it for about half an hour. The red segments are then scraped off the core and their woody centres separated out (preferably strained) to leave a thin, oily paste which looks like tomato sauce and has a distinctive, mildly astringent taste. It goes particularly well with pork, but is also eaten with greens and other vegetables. *Marita*

96

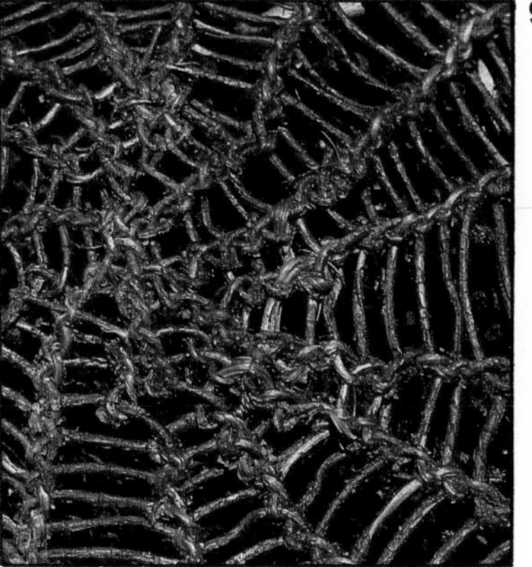
97

95

92
Coastal pandanus
93
Collecting *karuka*
94
Marita, Telefomin, West Sepik Province
95
Preparing a sauce from baked *marita* near Baktamin, Western Province
96
Coastal pandanus nuts
97
Woven basket containing *karuka*, Mount Hagen, Western Highlands Province

Polynesian chestnut

is uncommon in Port Moresby (I have bought it at Sogeri) and Rabaul, but is usually available in Lae and highlands markets from about December to March (and sometimes at other times). *Marita* oil is also used on the body and hair and for polishing arrow shafts.

Another, less common, species of pandanus is *P. foveolatus*, a high-altitude tree which yields a small nut either eaten raw, or cooked. Some other pandanus fruits are fed to pigs and cassowaries but not eaten by humans.

POLYNESIAN CHESTNUT

(p : *aila*) *Inocarpus fagifer I. edulus*

This is a tree which may grow as high as 20 metres, mostly along coastal areas. In Fiji, where the tree is common, it is called *ivi*. It has long, glossy, pale green leaves and a nut, surrounded by a hard husk, which is flattish, roughly oval and about 10 centimetres long.

The nuts may be green or, when older, yellowish brown; frequently when sold in the market the husk is brown and decayed, and the nut looks quite unappetizing. When baked or boiled, the kernel - if you can extract it from the tough husk - is sweet and dense, not unlike the European chestnut. Old nuts tend to be tough and in Polynesia are sometimes grated, mixed with coconut cream and baked in leaves.

TWO-LEAF (p : *tulip* ; m : *kemu*) *Gnetum gnemon*

The seed of the *tulip* looks like a small olive. When young the outer husk is green and can be easily split to obtain the juicy bean-like kernel, which may be eaten raw. When it is older, the husk turns red and hard and is usually cooked ; the cooked kernel tastes a little like an almond.

Pandanus fruit

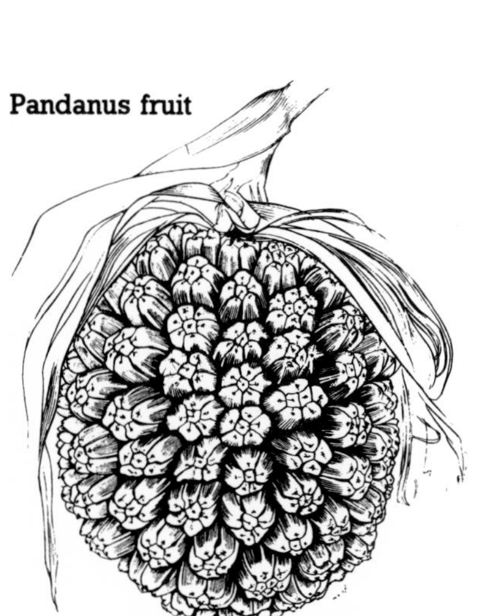

OKARI, INDIAN ALMOND, JAVA ALMOND

(p : *talis* ; m : *okari*) *Terminalia* spp.

The *okari (T. kaernbachii, T. okari*) is a tall tree of the lowland forests with large glossy leaves which turn red before falling. It produces large cigar-shaped nuts which are found seasonally in Port Moresby markets and may be eaten raw or cooked. *T. catappa*, the Indian almond or Java almond, is a popular tree in Port Moresby gardens; it yields a green-red-yellow almond-shaped fruit about 5-6 centimetres long whose rather astringent flesh is prized by flying foxes and small children and which contains a small kernel which may be eaten raw or cooked if you are energetic enough to extract it. *T. Impediens* also produces an edible nut. The nuts of some species of *Terminalia* must be washed and cooked before eating.

GALIP, PILI NUT (p : *galip* ; m : *ogaseva*) *Canarium* spp.

These nuts, from a tall lowland forest tree, are well known along the north coast, where they are still an important item of trade, and in the islands. The most common, *C. indicum*, has a hard outer shell, about the size of a walnut, which is in three segments. In the Sepik the segments are carved into miniature masks for tourists. The kernel is oily and aromatic.

(p : *salamon*) *Pangium edule*

This large bush tree produces a fruit which contains a number of large seeds that are quite an important food in several parts of the country. The seed, which has a brown skin and bright yellow flesh, contains cyanogenetic glucosides and requires careful preparation. The flesh can be cooked and is said to taste like passionfruit but the main food is the kernel, which is in two segments. Although boiling for a couple of hours is generally sufficient to render the seeds safe to eat, usually they are cooked (sometimes being crushed or cut up first) and then left in running water for anything from a day to several weeks. Alternatively the seeds are cooked and buried for some time. If immersed or buried the seeds ferment and the result is a fairly innocuous brown paste, which is sometimes recooked.

The unripe green fruit is used medicinally and the shells of the ripe seeds are commonly used as rattles.

99

100

98

98
Collecting Polynesian chestnuts, Tubetube, Milne Bay Province

99
Okari (*T. catappa*) nuts

100
Preparing *Pangium edule* seeds, Tauta, Morobe Province

101 103
Collecting lotus nuts, Isago lagoon, Western Province

102
Lotus nuts

CASTANOPSIS *Castanopsis acuminatissima*

This is an oak-like forest tree, fairly widespread in the highlands, which produces large quantities of small nuts similar in appearance to hazelnuts. *Castanopsis* may have been an important food of the early hunter-gatherers.

LOTUS NUTS (*Nelumbo nucifera*)

The pink or white flowering lotus plant is found in some swampy areas, notably the Chambri Lakes of the Sepik, Lake Murray and the lagoons of the Aramia River in the Western Province. The plant produces a broad, conical-shaped fruit containing numerous olive-shaped seeds. These seeds may be eaten raw or cooked. Raw they taste like beans; cooked they have a taste a little like almonds.

NIPA PALM (p : *wailsaksak* ; m : *biri*) *Nypa fruticans*

The seeds of the nipa palm contain a rather tasteless jelly which is sometimes eaten by people living in the swamps where the palm occurs.

BANANA, PLANTAIN (p : *banana* ; m : *biku*) *Musa* spp.

Bananas are the staple food of many people in coastal Papua and in the Markham valley, and an important supplementary

103

food in many other parts, growing up to an altitude of over 2000 metres. There is a large number of varieties of banana, many of which have been introduced since European contact; the Adzera people of the Markham valley have (at least) 36 words for banana. Some wild varieties, however, do not produce edible fruits.

Most are 'cooking' bananas, to be baked (in the skin) or (peeled) boiled, steamed or fried like root crops. They are starchy and dense and, especially when boiled, usually rather flavourless. Sweet 'eating' bananas are harder to find. The ability to distinguish 'cooking' from 'eating' bananas generally has to be acquired through trial and error, but any banana whose flesh is obviously soft (whether the skin is yellow or green) may be eaten raw, and very large or very pale yellow bananas are practically always for cooking. In some parts of the country, bananas are picked green and buried until the fruit ripens. The very large fruit of one variety (known in the Medlpa language as *ui pokau* or *ui mapugla*) is said to take years to ripen and is always cooked over the flames.

The dark purple inflorescence bud of the plant may also be eaten, boiled or baked, after the removal of the outer segments; it has a soft texture and a bitter-sweet taste. The young shoots of most species may be eaten like palm 'cabbage' and one species of banana (*M. sapientum var. Oleracea*) produces an edible rhizome.

104

105

106

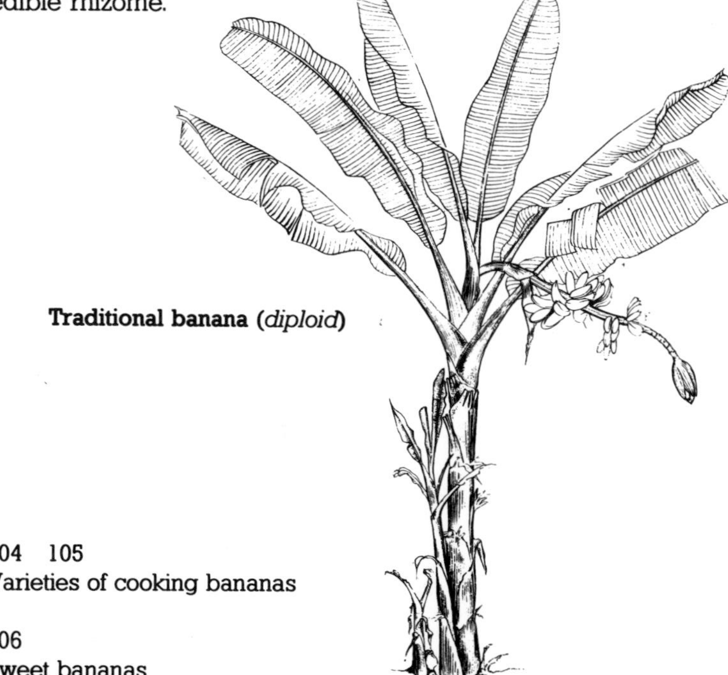

Traditional banana (*diploid*)

104 105
Varieties of cooking bananas

106
Sweet bananas

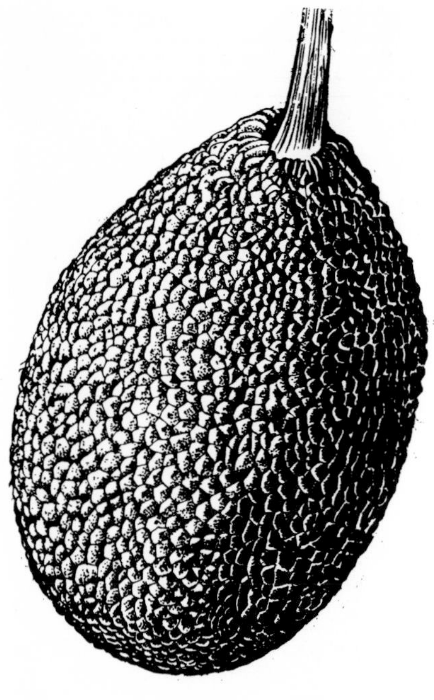

Breadfruit

BREADFRUIT (p : *kapiak* ; m : *unu*) *Artocarpus altilis A. incisus*

The fruit of this tree is a supplementary food in many parts of Papua New Guinea. The round green fruit, which may weigh up to about 5 kilograms is ready to eat when the flesh feels soft and a milky sap forms on the rind. The flesh is yellow and has a strong sweet smell. It may be eaten raw but is best baked whole on a fire or in an oven. The skin and seeds, if any, may then be removed and the flesh mashed. The flesh is rich and starchy. Alternatively, slice the not-quite-ripe fruit, soak in water for about thirty minutes, dry and use to make chips; or boil the fruit and cook with meat, or serve chilled as a salad. In parts of the Sepik a delicious 'bread' is made from breadfruit, grated coconut and sago, wrapped in leaves and cooked on an open fire.

Some fruit have seeds about the size and texture of chestnuts; these seeds taste rather like young potatoes, though more dense. They may be eaten straight out of the baked fruit or (preferably) roasted lightly over a fire. In parts of the highlands, people eat the seeds and throw the rest of the fruit away. The cooked seeds are often seen in markets and in most places twenty toea worth is a fair meal.

In parts of Polynesia, breadfruit is fermented in large pits lined with leaves and preserved for consumption over several years.

WILD FIGS (p : *kombi* ; m : *korukoru*) *Ficus* spp.

Nearly all species of *Ficus* (which belongs to the same family - *Moraceae* as the breadfruit) yield edible green leaves (see above) or fruit. Usually the fruit of *Ficus* is a bush food and not a regular part of the diet. The only fruits I have tasted were dry and had little flavour. They can be very astringent. Those recorded as being eaten include *F. botryocarpa,* which yields small figs; *F. copiosa; F. cynaroides; F. dammaropsis; F. itoana* (which has a cauliflower like fruit); *F. pungens; F. virgata* and *F. wassa.*

MANGROVE (p : *mangro* ; m : *gavera*) *Bruguiera* spp.

In some coastal areas the germinating seeds of the mangrove are eaten, mostly as a famine food. The long, cigar-shaped 'fruit' (technically, propagules) are first boiled and the softened skin scraped off. The propagule is then cut into pieces and soaked in salt water until soft, in the process getting rid of excessive tannin. Finally the water is squeezed out to leave a coarse brown mash which is mostly starch and has little flavour.

107
Breadfruit seeds and breadfruit-coconut 'bread' on sale in Maprik, East Sepik Province

108
Breadfruit

109
Wild figs

110
Mangrove propagules

107 

108 

 109

 110

PAWPAW, PAPAYA (p: *popo*; m: *loku, nita*) *Carica papaya*

Pawpaw, though apparently a recent introduction from tropical America is now a common tree in lowlands gardens and bush. The fruit is usually available in markets - even though hotels in Port Moresby frequently tell guests that they cannot have pawpaw for breakfast because it is 'out of season'.

The ripe, orange fruit, seeds removed, is best eaten fresh, though some prefer to add lime juice. Particularly sweet are the long fruit which have a red flesh. The unripe fruit may also be eaten, baked or boiled; the last is a little like pumpkin but more moist. The green fruit is a meat tenderiser. If you really want to get the most out of the pawpaw tree, you may also eat the leaves (see p. 58), the flowers, and use the seeds as a laxative.

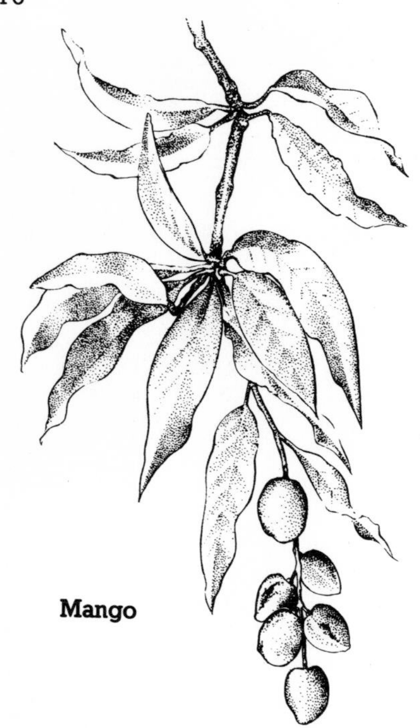
Mango

MANGO (p : *mango* ; m : *vaivai*) *Mangifera* spp.

Some species of mango (*M. minor* and *M. foetida*) appear to be indigenous to Papua New Guinea, but the fruits of these are fibrous and taste of turpentine. The best tasting fruit is that of *M. indica*, which has been introduced from Asia. The fruit grows on a large tree and is seasonal. Unripe (as they generally seem to be in the markets) the green fruit may be used (non-traditionally) to make sauces or chutney. The ripe, green or yellow fruit are eaten fresh and commonly used for jams and chutney. In India the dried kernels of the fruit are sometimes made into flour.

GUAVA (p : *yambo* ; m : *guava*) *Psidium guajava*

This is a green or yellow fruit, about the size of a passionfruit with pink flesh, hard seeds and a strong smell which most people find objectionable. It is an introduced fruit which occurs, seasonally, in most lowlands markets, though it is often unripe when sold. The fruit may be eaten fresh and stewed ; it has a high pectin content which is good for making jam. The strawberry guava (*P. cattleianum*), produces a smaller fruit which is red or yellow when ripe and much sweeter than *P. guajava*.

Fivecorner

FIVECORNER, STAR FRUIT, CARAMBOLA (p : *faivkorn*) *Averrhoa carambola*

The fivecorner is a native of Indonesia and appears to be a relatively recent introduction to Melanesia. It is a greenish-orange fruit, about 10-15 centimetres long, with a distinctive shape which accounts for its English name. The flesh is crisp, juicy and tart. Use sparingly in fruit salad or use, sweetened, to make a refreshing drink.

ROSE APPLE (p : *laulau*) *Syzygium jambos*

The rose apple is similar in colour to the related Malay apple, but is larger and more rounded and its flesh is drier. The fruit can be eaten fresh or used to make a pleasant drink.

Until recently, species of *Syzygium* were regarded as members of a larger genus, *Eugenia*. Some other species of *Eugenia* also produce edible fruit, among them *E. tierneyana* which bears a small red fleshy fruit which has a sharp taste.

111

MALAY APPLE (p : *laulau*) *Syzygium malaccense*

The Malay apple is a small, pear-shaped, bright pink, red or white fruit with a crisp but light white flesh which is faintly sweet and aromatic. It is found seasonally in lowlands markets, and is best eaten fresh.

TAUN (p : *taun* ; m : *okamu*) *Pometia pinnata*

This common lowlands tree produces an edible fruit about the size of a small plum, which may be green, red or black. It is especially popular among the Boiken people of the East Sepik, who used to hold annual *taun* festivals. There is a semi-cultivated form of *taun* which has much larger fruits than the wild plant ; it is found, seasonally, in the Kavieng and Rabaul markets, and also in Fiji.

112

CUSTARD APPLE *Annona squamosa*

The custard apple is an exotic, sweet fruit about the size of an apple; it comprises a number of segments of delicious soft white flesh around the large black seeds. It will be found, seasonally, in lowlands markets.

BUKBUK (p : *bukbuk*) *Burckella obovata*

This is a delicious fruit, about the size of an apple, which grows on a tall forest tree. It has a bright green soft skin, and white flesh with a single almond-shaped seed. The fruit, when ripe, has the texture of an avocado and a delicate flavour somewhat like a custard apple, but less sweet. I first came across it several years ago on Panaeate, Milne Bay Province, where it is called *kapoi*. It appears to be common in Milne Bay; I have also found it near Finschhafen, and am told that it grows in Rabaul, whence the name *bukbuk*.

113

GARCINIA (p : *pota*) *Garcinia* spp.

I have never in Papua New Guinea, come across the purple fruit of the mangosteen (*G. mangostana*), the sweet exotic fruit common in southeast Asia, though I understand it has been introduced in the Lae and Rabaul areas (the latter, pre-1940). But other species of *Garcinia* appear to be indigenous. In the Samarai market I have bought a small, yellow, round *garcinia* fruit with a sweet pulpy centre.

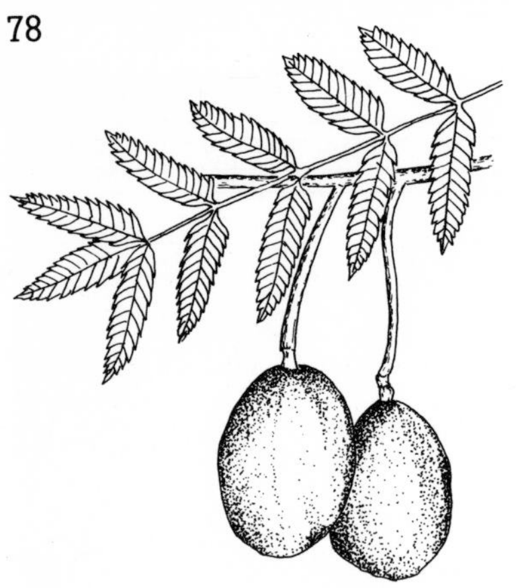

Spondias dulcis

(*previous page*)
111
Malay apple (*laulau*)

112
Fivecorner fruit

113
Burkella obovata, Paneate, Milne Bay Province

114
Soursop

115
Indian mulberry

116
Rosella

POLYNESIAN PLUM, HOG PLUM, TAHITIAN APPLE, VENUS APPLE *Spondias dulcis*

This tall tree yields a small, yellow, pear-shaped fruit with a prickly seed, which is firm, juicy, aromatic and slightly acid. The fruit is well known in Fiji (where it is known as *wi*) but in Papua New Guinea, apparently, is seldom eaten (though it is relished by pigs and cassowaries).

SOURSOP (p : *sauasap, sapsap*) *Annona muricata*

The soursop is related to the custard apple and somewhat similar in composition. It is a large fruit, whose smooth green skin is covered with small, soft spines. It has more flesh than the custard apple and is more tart. Like the custard apple it is an introduced plant.

INDIAN MULBERRY *Morinda citrifolia*

The *Morinda citrifolia* is a small tree with broad shiny leaves. It produces a pale yellowish green fruit, about the shape of a pine cone, which when ripe has a white, almost transparent flesh and smells like Camembert cheese. The fruit is considered poisonous unless absolutely ripe. A nutrition survey report in 1947 described the fruit as having 'a disgusting smell and taste, but....considered palatable by the natives'. The taste is somewhere between a Camembert and a custard apple. It appears to be mainly a famine food. The young leaves may be eaten, and the bark and roots of the tree are used to make dyes.

ROSELLA, RED SORRELL *Hibiscus sabdariffa*

This is a bush with dark green serrated leaves and yellow flowers. The red shiny calyx (which I have seen in the Wewak market) can be used to make tea, syrup or jelly. The young leaves may also be eaten. The plant, which seems to have originated in West Africa, is probably a recent introduction.

AMOMUM *Amomum* spp.

Amomum is a large herb which is cultivated as a boundary marker. Its fruits are sometimes eaten as a snack. They are said to taste a little like passionfruit.

PASSIONFRUITS *Passiflora* spp.

114

There are several species of passionfruit in Papua New Guinea, all recently introduced (the plant is a native of South America) but some are now growing wild. The fruit grow profusely on vines.

The most frequently found is the dark purple, egg-shaped passionfruit (*P. edulis*). This was introduced as a cash crop in the Eastern Highlands and is now plentiful - and cheap - in most highland markets. There is also a yellow species (*P. flavicarpa*) which is found in lowlands, and sometimes in highlands markets ; often this plant is wild or semi-cultivated. The yellow fruit usually have less flavour.

Also common in the highlands is the banana passionfruit or tacsonia (*P. mollissima*), a somewhat longer yellow fruit (hence the name) which, like the passionfruit, consists almost entirely of sweet fleshy seeds but has a more subtle flavour. In the early 1970s it was almost impossible to drive between Goroka and Kundiawa without being stopped by hordes of children selling banana passionfruit.

115

The granadilla (*P. laurifolia*) and giant granadilla (*P. quadrangularis*) are larger, green fruits similar in structure, with a slightly tart but unmistakably 'tropical' flavour. The fleshy skin of the giant granadilla can be cooked and used as a dessert ; it is sometimes used as a substitute for apple in 'apple' pie.

P. foetida is a small, yellow or orange fruit, covered with a fluffy green leaf-like structure which occurs wild. The unripe fruit are cyanogenetic and the plant is best avoided.

CITRUS FRUITS *Citrus* spp.

116

There are numerous citrus fruits cultivated or growing wild in Papua New Guinea. The only truly indigenous citrus is the bush orange (*C. papuana*) which is an orange with a green skin. It is somewhat tart. Limes (*C. aurantifolia, C. acida*) and lemons (*C. limon*) (p : *muli ;* m : *siporo*) are fairly common in lowlands markets. Other lesser known but fairly common citrus fruits are the pomelo or shaddock (*C. grandis, C. decumana* or *C. maxima*), a large grapefruit-like fruit with pinkish flesh which may be eaten fresh or used for making jam, and the citron (*C. medica*), a large lemon-shaped fruit with a thick skin which in Europe is used mostly for the peel (and in Corsica for making a sweet liqueur).

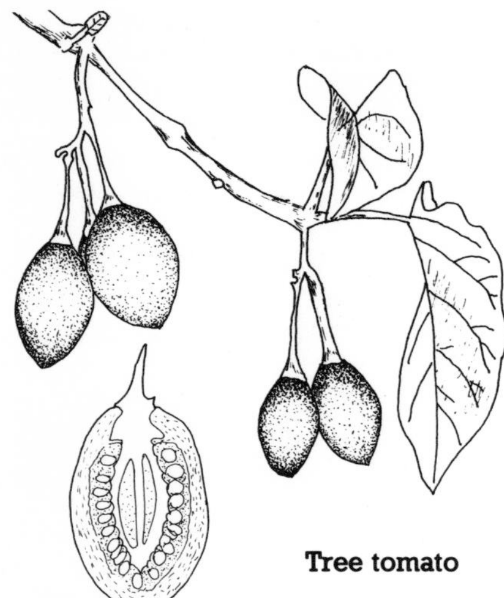
Tree tomato

TREE TOMATO, TAMARILLO *Cyphomandra betacea*

The tree tomato, a native of Peru, is a red fruit with black seeds, like a cross between a tomato and a passionfruit. Although recently introduced, it has become common in highlands markets. Eat it fresh, as a fruit or added to salads, or steamed.

WILD BERRIES *Rubus* spp and others

In the Eastern Highlands I have come across a small wild berry (*?Rubus rosaefolius*). It produces a small red berry (rather like a strawberry in appearance) which is watery but sweet. I was told that some people eat them.

Rubus moluccanus, a woody ground vine with red berries, has also been recorded as a food, but not esteemed.

117

117
Barringtonia spp.

OTHER INTRODUCED FRUITS

Other fruits which have been introduced and may occasionally be encountered in markets or suburban or station gardens, are the pomegranate (*Punica granatum*) ; velvet apple or butter fruit (*Diospyros discolor*) ; durian (*Durio zibethinus*) ; rambutan (*Nephelium lappaceum*) ; langsat (*Lansium domesticum*) ; and jackfruit (*Artocarpus integrifolia*). The yellow-red fruit of the cashew nut tree (*Anarcardium occidentale*) - called cashew apple - is also very pleasant to eat (though the appended seed is toxic if not cooked) ; the fruit has a subtle, slightly astringent flavour. And of course there is the avocado (*Persea gratissima*), fruit of the Aztecs, which grows wild around Rabaul and is becoming increasingly common in the highlands. Most of these plants are available from the Lowlands Agricultural Experiment Station at Kerevat.

Other recorded fruits and nuts, mostly indigenous or early introductions, and usually regarded as bush foods, include the folowing. (Again the list is largely from Straatman's checklist.)

Achras zapota — the sapodilla or chico, a tree with sweet egg-shaped fruits which have a thin brown skin.

Aleurites moluccana — the candlenut (Motu, *omo*) kernel edible if cooked.

Antidesma bunius — the currant tree; a small tree which bears small, cream, red or purple fruits which have an acid pulp.

Avicenna sp. — a mangrove plant with edible seeds.

Barringtonia spp. — a family of trees whose nuts are a common food, raw or cooked, both in the highlands and on the coast. A coastal species (*? B. edulus*), in Pidgin *pau* and known in Fiji as *vutu*, produces clusters of green fruit which contain a delicious kernel not unlike an *okari* nut. Some species of *Barringtonia*, however, contain saponins and are commonly used as fish poisons.

Coccoloba uvifera — the seaside grape, a small tree with an astringent fruit.

Cycas circinalis — a starch may be extracted from the seeds of this tree but the seeds must be carefully prepared (they are usually prepared in much the same way as *Pangium edule* nuts); the fermented cycad seeds are said to smell like old German cheese.

Dillena spp. — a family of shrubs and small trees which produce a tart fruit.

Dracontomelum mangiferum — the New Guinea walnut; produces seeds with edible flesh.

Ehretia microphylla — a small shrub with an edible round yellow fruit.

Elaeocarpus spp. — a forest tree which produces edible nuts.

Finschia chloroxantha — a forest tree which produces an edible brown kidney-shaped seeds. Other species of *Finschia* may also produce edible seeds.

Flacourtia rukam — the Indian plum; a red berry, bitter but edible raw and cooked.

Freycinetia spp. — forest tree which produces edible fruit.

Heritiera littoralis — a plant of the mangrove swamps, with edible seeds.

Madhuca sp. — a tree with fleshy fruits.

Moringa oleifera — the horseradish tree (whose leaves, also, are eaten).

Muntingia calabura — (Pidgin: *kirsen*) the Jamaican cherry or Panama berry; a small tree, common in gardens around the country, which produces a small, sweet, red fruit which is full of little soft seeds.

Nephelium spp. — a genus of trees which includes the rambutan and lychee.

Parsonia sp. — produces edible seeds.

Phalena papuana — a small shrub which produces a sweet fruit.

Physalis peruviana — the cape gooseberry; an introduced plant whose small yellow fruit are edible.

Pithecellobium dulce — a small tree with an edible fruit.

Solanum nodiflorum — black nightshade; the small berries of this plant may be eaten when they are ripe (black). They are sweet but without a strong flavour. The green berries contain toxic alkaloid.

Sonneratia sp. — another mangrove plant which produces edible fruit.

Sterculia spp. — forest trees; *S. quadrifida* (the peanut tree) produces bright orange pods which contain black seeds, and are edible raw or cooked. The seeds of *S. foetida* are also edible but only after cooking.

Ximenia americana — a small coastal tree known variously as yellow plum, wild olive or wild lime. It produces a yellow plum-like fruit with a large stone and a very acid flesh. (In South Africa the fruit is used to make a kind of beer.)

Zingiber minor — a wild ginger whose seeds are eaten and said to be crisp and sweet.

OTHER EDIBLE PLANTS

Sugar cane

SUGAR CANE (p : *suga* ; m : *tohu*) *Saccharum officinarum*

Sugar cane is indigenous to Papua New Guinea : indeed Melanesian plants seem to have provided the basic stock for a large part of the world's commercial sugar plantations. Most gardens, up to 2500 metres, contain some sugar cane. Usually it is eaten as a snack between meals, by stripping the outside skin and chewing a length of the stalk. It quenches the thirst and provides energy, especially on long walks.

In southeast Asia it is common to see street vendors extracting the juice from cane by pushing lengths of cane through a small manual mill. This provides a refreshing long drink and the juice may be heated to obtain crude sugar.

LOWLAND PITPIT (p : *pitpit* ; m : *godibu*) *Saccharum edule*

This plant is related to sugar cane but is cultivated for the unopened bud of its inflorescences. These inflorescences, which are about the size and shape of bullrushes, do not normally emerge from their grassy sheath, and in the market are usually sold in a bundle tied together by the top of the sheaths. *Pitpit* may be baked steamed or boiled ; occasionally it is eaten raw. Its flavour is improved by the addition of plenty of coconut cream, or butter and lemon juice.

Job's tears

JOB'S TEARS (p : *karapa*) *Coix lacryma-jobi*

The grey and white seeds of this grass are used ornamentally in many parts of Papua New Guinea - and most spectacularly in the mourning dress of the Okapa people of the Eastern Highlands - and are now frequently used in necklaces made for tourists. Although not widely recognised as a food in Papua New Guinea, the seeds can be crushed to provide a nutritious cereal. (There is evidence that Job's tears were an important food in Asia before the spread of rice).

LEMON GRASS *Cymbopogon citratus*

Lemon grass occurs fairly widely in Papua New Guinea. It appears to be an introduced plant though it was reported as being used as a flavouring by the New Guinea Nutrition Survey Expedition in 1947, and is also used in magic.

Lemon grass is, of course, an important ingredient in southeast Asian cooking and may be used to make a delicious tea. For cooking use a small quantity of the soft white base of the leaves.

BIXA, ANNATTO *Bixa orellana*

Annatto is an essential ingredient in a good deal of Caribbean and Filipino cooking. A red oil is made by stirring the fresh seeds of the bixa plant into oil or fat.

The bixa is a traditional plant of Papua New Guinea, and the small red seeds which are found in the furry, brown heart-shaped seed pod have long been used (as they were used also by the American Indians) as a face and body paint.

As far as I know, the plant has never been used in traditional cooking but is often found growing around villages and in suburban gardens and is well worth trying. (See chapter six).

FUNGI (p: *talinga, papai*) Various

In the Sepik (and probably elsewhere), people eat a pink fungus which grows on the debris left after sago preparation, and in the foothills of the Finisterre Ranges I have seen people collect both a pink fungus growing on rotten tree trunks, and a greyish mushroom which looked like a common field mushroom. All of these fungi were lightly cooked over an open fire before eating. Unfortunately, none of them were identified, but species of fungi which have been reported as being eaten in Papua New Guinea, include *Agaricus, Auricularia, Clitocybe, Pleurotus* and *Polyporus.*

Among the Kuma people of the Wahgi Valley, the eating of certain species of fungi (known in the Middle Wahgi language as *nonda* and identified as species of *Boletus* and *Russula*) induces a state of 'mushroom madness' in some of the consumers. Men become aggressive and women flirtatious.

SEAWEED Various

A pale green leafy *Ulva* is an occasional item of diet for coastal people in Milne Bay, and probably in other provinces. The sea grape (*Caulerpa* sp.) is eaten on the north coast. Many other seaweeds are edible but do not appear to have been a part of traditional diets.

118
Bixa orellana

119
Fungus (*polyporus* sp.)

SEAFOODS

120
Collecting shellfish, Goodenough Island, Milne Bay Province

121
Shellfish (*Atactodea striata*)

120

121

122
Mudcrabs
123
Freshwater crayfish, Wasapea, Western Province
124
Reef fish and lobster

(*overleaf*)
125
Smoked *tilapia*
126
Shark meat
127
A catch of eels near Ruti, Western Highlands Province

MOLLUSCS

I have been told that all shellfish are normally edible, even those cone shells which can inflict a poisonous bite. The only reservation is that during 'red tides', certain bivalves may become toxic. Indeed, a great variety of the shellfish occurring in Papua New Guinea waters, and a number of freshwater molluscs are eaten - raw, boiled or baked.

Along the southern Papuan coast, the more popular saltwater shellfish include (with Motu names, where known, in brackets) oysters (*siro, batata*), mussels (*dihudihu, gogodiro*), cockle (*kwadi*), thorny oyster or spondylus (*sisihu*), conch (*kibi*), spider shell (*ragaraga*), volute (*koko*), olive (*digoa*), cowrie (*nononono*), stromb and mud whelk. Other important food shells in Papua New Guinea are the giant turban shell (often misleadingly referred to as the 'green snail' shell) (Pidgin *talipun* ; *Turbo marmoratus*), and the clam or *Tridacna* (Pidgin *kramsel*), the largest species of which may yield over 200 kilograms of meat. Squid (Pidgin *tauka*) are also eaten.

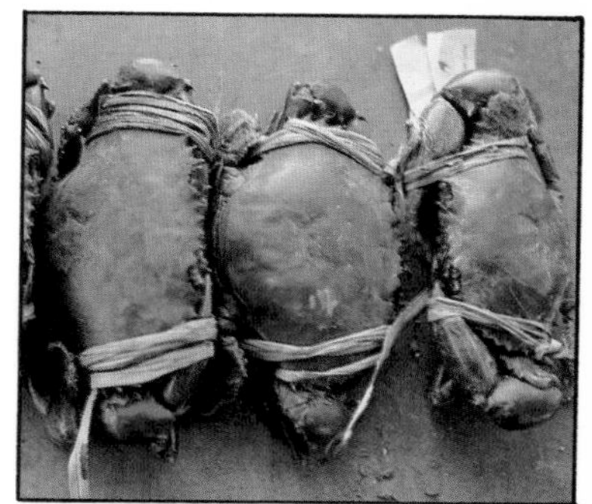

122

Several species of land snails (p: *demdem;* m: *kururu*) are eaten. A small land snail is especially popular among the Orokaiva of Oro Province. However, the giant snail, a native of Africa introduced by the Japanese, and now a common garden pest, is not eaten. The widespread belief that the snail was brought to Papua New Guines as a food is, according to one authority on the subject, erroneous.

CRUSTACEANS

Crayfish (p: *kindam;* m: *ura ; Panulirus* spp.) are plentiful, at the right time of the year, along many parts of the Papua New Guinea coastline; there was, in the 1970s, a commercial industry (based on *P. ornatus*) on Yule Island in the Central Province. Around October to January, one can often purchase lobsters - cooked or fresh - at the Gordons market in Port Moresby. Freshwater crayfish (*Cherax* spp.), some of which grow up to about 2 kilograms also occur in some lakes and streams.

123

A great variety of crabs (p: *kuka ;* m: *bava, dubara, kokopa*), saltwater and freshwater, is found in Papua New Guinea and many species are eaten. In Port Moresby markets one may find the large purple-blue mud crabs (Motu, *bava; Scylla serrata*) which live among the mangroves. The large robber or coconut crab (*Birgus* spp.), which is prized in Vanuatu for its tasty meat and coconut filled 'sac', occurs on a few small islands.

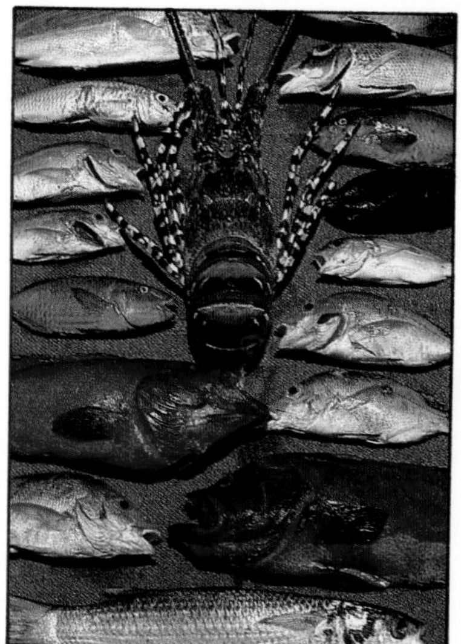

124

Several species of marine and freshwater prawns (p: *kindam;* m: *pai*) are eaten. Freshwater prawns are a popular food along the Sepik River, and the Papuan Gulf supports a commercial industry.

Traditionally, crustaceans are usually baked on an open fire, and sometimes the outer shell, softened by cooking, is eaten with the flesh.

FISH

Considering the great profusion of fish in Papua New Guinean waters, it is surprisingly difficult to obtain fresh fish unless you catch your own. By no means are all of Papua New Guinea's

125

126

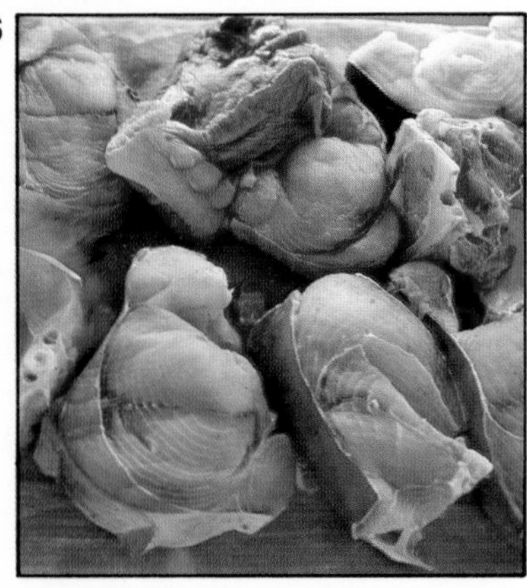

127

coastal dwellers, active fishermen. However, in Port Moresby it is usually possible to get a reasonable selection of fresh reef fish (and sometimes tuna, mackerel and turtle), in Koki and Gordons markets late on Thursday and Friday afternoon, and urban supermarkets often have frozen barramundi and highlands trout. In Rabaul, fish can sometimes be purchased along the north coast road.

Among the best eating fish of coastal waters are coral trout, rock cod, sea perch, bream, sweetlip, emperor, parrotfish, rainbowfish, wrasse, jewfish, unicornfish, mullet, trevally, tuna, mackerel, barracuda, longtom and garfish. Coral trout (*bikmaus ; balala*), the yellow and blue sea perch (Motu *bonohir*), parrotfish (various Motu names), and longtom (*longpela maus ; kwarabada*) are fairly common in Port Moresby markets. The most common freshwater fish are now carp and *tilapia* (Pidgin *makau*), both introduced, though freshwater eels (p : *maleo ;* m : *dagwala*) and catfish (Pidgin *mausgras*) are an important supplentary food in some parts of the country. Trout have recently been introduced commercially in the Eastern Highlands.

The barramundi (Motu *anama*) spends part of its life in freshwater and part in saltwater. (It also changes sex during its life cycle). Between November and March, large numbers are found in the bays and estuaries around the mouth of the Fly River, where they spawn before returning upriver. It is an excellent table fish, especially when caught in saltwater.

,A few fish in Papua New Guinea waters are poisonous. These include several species of the order *Tetrodontiformes* (toadfish, pufferfish, porcupinefish, filefish, triggerfish and boxfish) but you will not find these in a market and most fishermen know them. Some other normally edible fish (generally only fish over 10 kilograms) have also been known to have caused poisoning after feeding on a certain algae. This includes red emperor, red bass, coral trout, coral cod and trevally.

Munro's *Fishes of New Guinea* provides an exhaustive description of Papua New Guinea's fishes and is a valuable guide to identifying fish caught or bought in the market. Personal tastes differ and it is worth trying a variety, including smoked *tilapia* and, even better, smoked reef fish.

OTHER SEAFOOD

Octopus (p : *kurita* : m : *urita, dune, managi*) is often eaten and sea urchins are eaten raw among some coastal people. Sea slugs (trepang, bêche-de-mer) (Pidgin *pislama*) used to be collected along the Papua coast and dried for export to Asia, and were occasionally eaten by local people.

MEAT

As one early European observer said (of the Mailu people): 'So long as it is flesh, and can be got, everything is brought to the larder'. It is not my intention to encourage the consumption of Papua New Guinea's wild creatures, many of which - including the dugong, turtle, cuscus, echidna and several species of birds - deserve protection. However, for the record, I have included under 'meat' all those animals, birds and smaller creatures known to serve as food.

Methods of cooking animals and birds may vary from place to place and according to the beast. In general, however, both are generally cooked lightly over a fire (birds are plucked first), the innards then removed for separate cooking, and the cooking of the animal or bird completed on the fire or in a pot or bamboo.

Usually both flesh and edible offal are eaten and the distribution of meat follows a set of entrenched social conventions and taboos - normally ensuring that the older men get the best parts of the meat. Often the smaller animals and insects are eaten only by women and children.

PEOPLE (p : *birua ;* m : *tau anina*) *Homo sapiens*

Before European contact, cannibalism was common in many parts of the country. It was vigorously opposed by the church and secular officials and is now a thing of the past. The last reliably reported case of cannibalism was in 1971, when seven men from the Western Province were charged with improperly and indecently interfering with a corpse (they had cooked and eaten with sago, the bodies of two men who had been murdered by others); they were acquitted, a Supreme Court Judge ruling that this was normal and reasonable behaviour for them.*

Cannibalism frequently had important ritual significance, but it also appears to have appealed on gastronomic grounds, and human flesh was probably a significant source of protein in some areas, especially in times of general food shortage. On the other hand, it is now believed that cannibalism was associated with the spread, among the Fore people of the Eastern Highlands, of the disease *kuru*, a virus being transmitted through consumption of the dead person's brain during mourning rites.

Few recipes for human flesh have been recorded, but it seems to have been cooked like any other meat and was generally

*In August 1978 three young men of the Western Province were sentenced to 15 months' jail for eating part of the legs of a dead man.

128

128
Cooking pig in an earth oven, Daulo, Eastern Highlands Province

preferred to pig. Hides recorded in 1939 (*Beyond the Kubea*) that people of the Strickland River did not eat the legs of men : 'They ate only that portion above the hips, which tasted like opossum. The body of a victim was singed over the fire like a pig, so that the top layer of skin could be removed; then it was cut into strips, some roasted plainly on the open fire, others cooked in bamboo with bush cabbage'. Old men among the Adzera of the Markham valley, once renowned for their headhunting and cannibalism, recall that the most favoured cuts of human meat were the feet and hands, while the Keraki of the Western Province are recorded as favouring eyeballs and snippets of cheek. One tribe of the Orokaiva is said to have taken slices off a living victim for periods of up to a week, and also to have relished fresh brains. Along the Sepik River, where homicidal cults flourished, I have been told that human heads were often boiled with *balbal*.

129
Singeing the hairs of a pig prior to cooking, Yabominu, East Sepik Province

130
Cutting up pig, Yabominu, East Sepik Province

131
Exchanging pig meat, Wabag, Enga Province

129

130

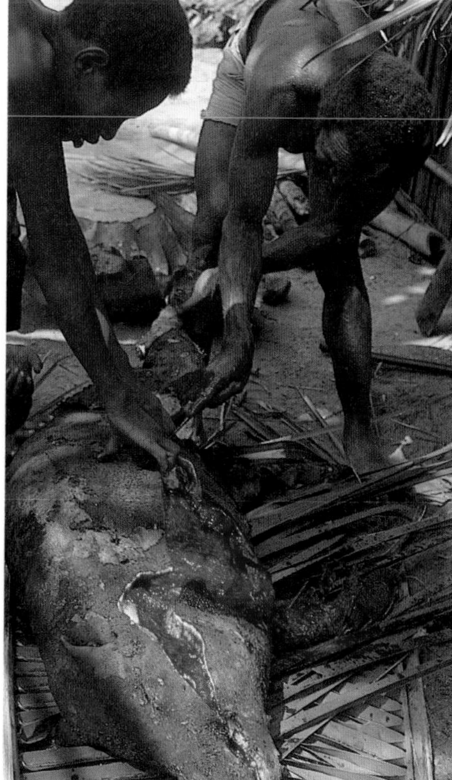

131

PIG (p : *pik*; m : *boroma*) *Sus scofia*

The pig was probably introduced to Papua New Guinea by early immigrants some 6 000 years ago. Apart from recently introduced animals, the pig, dog and fowl are the only domesticated animals in Papua New Guinea society. Feral pigs (*Sus scrofia papuensis*) are also hunted. As well as being a source of food, and a significant source of protein, the pig has an important place in the social, economic and religious systems of most traditional communities. In the highlands, formal pig killings and exchanges may involve the slaughtering at a single time, of several thousand pigs. Pigs are used to buy wives and land; to pay debts and fines. They are a measure of wealth and social status. In some parts of the country the pig is treated as a member of the family; the anthropologist F.E. Williams, once wrote that 'the principal sources of joy and dissension in the life of Orokolo males are their women and their pigs'. In the highlands, orphaned piglets may be suckled by the women, along with their children, and women have been known to cut off a finger joint as a sign of mourning for a dead pig.

Pig is commonly cooked in earth ovens, together with tubers and greens, but may also be cooked directly on the fire or, in portions, steamed or boiled in bamboo or pots. All parts, except the gall bladder, are normally eaten. Despite the social and economic importance of the pig, however, its contribution to village diets, even in the highlands, is small.

Reasonable caution should be exercised in eating pig. I was advised not to eat pig in the field, by a seasoned agricultural extension officer. For a start, he said, village pigs are often diseased, and also, the conditions under which they are killed often leave something to be desired. Cooking, he went on, rather than killing off bacteria, frequently simply raises the temperature of the meat to a level at which the bacteria flourish. The fact that, in food exchanges, the cooked meat is often handled by a number of people over several days adds to the risk, and finally, if the pork is taken with quantities of *kaukau* and taro, these tend to stop up the bowels, giving toxins extra time to make their presence felt. Deaths from *'pig bel'*, an infection of the upper bowel, often follow pig feasts. All this notwithstanding, village-cooked pork can be delicious and I have eaten if often without any ill effects. Indeed, pig well cooked in an earth oven (a particular speciality of the Tolai) is hard to beat.

DOG (p : *dok ;* m : *sisia*) *Canis familaris C. hallstromi*

Traditionally, dogs were eaten in several communities, but with other sources of protein now more readily available, this practice seems to have become less common. Dogs were cooked in much the same way as pigs.

WALLABY (p : *sikau ;* m : *magani*) *Thylogale bruijni* and others

Wallaby is a common game animal found in most parts of the country, and lightly cooked wallaby is often on sale in Port Moresby markets. The flesh is tough and a little like rabbit in taste.

FLYING FOX
(p : *blakbokis ;* m : *mariboi*) *Dobsonia moluccensis*

This large, fruit-eating bat is a common item of food in many parts of the country. Outside Wewak, it is not uncommon to see large flying fox nets hanging across cleared flight paths by the side of the road, and flying foxes are common items in the Wewak and Maprik markets.

132
Smoked wallaby

132 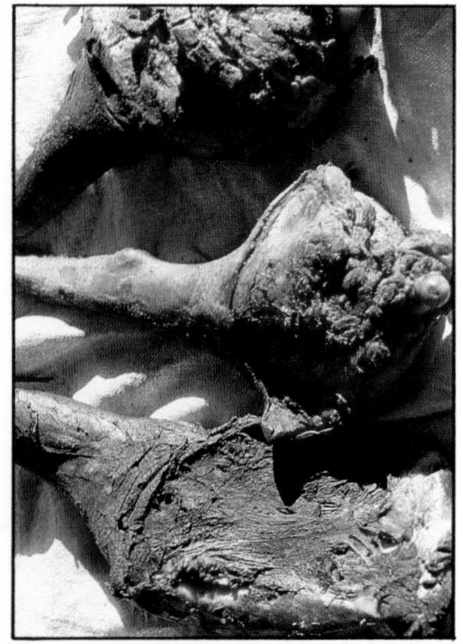

Flying fox meat is a delicacy. The flesh is sometimes compared with chicken but is in fact rather rich and more like a game bird.

Usually the animal is cooked over an open fire so that the fur is singed off and the skin is removed before eating. Sometimes the animal is gutted before cooking. In some parts of the country the whole animal is boiled and eaten fur, bones and all (only the gall bladder being rejected). Fortunately I have never been offered flying fox cooked this way, but someone who has, described the taste as '...well, furry'.

Few expatriates in Papua New Guinea seem to have tasted flying fox though in New Caledonia the flesh is highly esteemed by French *colons*.

OTHER FURRED (AND SPINEY) ANIMALS

It is safe to say that all other furred animals occurring in Papua New Guinea are eaten from time to time somewhere in the country, and it is not intended here to give a complete list of the country's fauna (such a list may be found in the *Encyclopaedia of Papua New Guinea*). The more common food animals, however, are listed below. Many of the smaller animals are commonly eaten only by women and children. Methods of cooking vary, but the most common method is probably cooking directly over an open fire.

Tree kangaroo (p: *sikau*; m: *au magani*) *Dendrolagus* spp.
Cuscus (p: *kapul*; m: *varua*) *Phalanger* spp.
Possum (p: *kapul*; m: *diredire*) *Pseudocheirus* spp. and others.

133
Cuscus

134
Skinning a cuscus in the bush near Seltamin, Western Province

133

134

Bandicoot (p : *mumut ;* m : *mada*) *Echymipera* spp., *Peroyctes* spp. *Isoodon* spp.

Bush rat (p : *rat ;* m : *bita*) *Rattus* spp., *Uromys* spp., *Melomys* spp. and others. The giant rat *Melomys rothschildi* is especially prized.

Bats (p : *blakbokis ; liklik blakbokis ;* m : *maragi, sisiboi*) Various. In addition to the flying fox, large fruit-eating bats of the genus *Pteropus* are popular food.

Echidna *Zaglossus bruijni*, *Tachyglossus aculeatus*

135 

135
Tortoises, Angoram market, East Sepik Province

TURTLE AND TORTOISE

(p : *trausel ;* m : *matabudi* [sea turtle], *gero* [tortoise]) Various

The big sea turtles are a much sought after food, especially in Western Papua. The most common as a food is the green turtle (*Chelonia mydas*) which grows up to about a metre in length. The hawksbill (*Eretmochelys imbricata*) is also fairly common and its shell is widely used in traditional jewelry. Other members of the *Cheloniidae* family, and also the huge leathery turtle (*Dermochelys coriacea*), are found in Papua New Guinea waters - though some species in seriously declining numbers - and several freshwater turtles and tortoises occur in lowlands lakes and streams. I have seen saltwater turtle on sale in markets in Port Moresby, Rabaul and Daru and tortoises in Port Moresby and Angoram.

Sometimes tortoises and turtles are cooked whole; the shell is broken open and the meat and juices eaten from the shell. Otherwise they are cut up and distributed and baked or boiled in pieces. Turtle meat is very fatty and in the case of the green turtle is greenish. The white meat tastes a little like veal.

Turtle eggs (saltwater turtles lay between 50 and 200 little round leather-shelled eggs) are a delicacy and are sometimes available in Rabaul and Lae markets.

DUGONG

(p : *bonon ;* m : *rui*) *Dugong dugon*

The dugong is now a protected species and its numbers appear to be declining. However it may still be caught by traditional methods and I have seen dugong meat on sale in the Daru market. An adult dugong may reach a length of about 4 metres and a girth of over 2 metres. The flesh is said to taste a little like beef, but with a fishy flavour.

CROCODILE

(p : *pukpuk ;* m : *huala*) *Crocodylus* spp.

Freshwater and estuarine crocodiles are a fairly common

source of meat, especially to people in the swampy areas of the Gulf and Western Provinces and the Sepik. The flesh is usually baked or boiled. It is rather fatty and has a strong fishy flavour. I have been told that if people eat large crocodiles they acquire a strong and unpleasant body odour which lasts for several days, but I have not had the opportunity to test this.

Crocodile eggs are regarded as something of a delicacy. The eggs boiled are said to have a creamy consistency.

LIZARDS (p : *pilai* ; m : *hariha*) Various

Most species of lizard seem to be eaten, the smaller ones mostly by children. Goannas (*Varanus* spp.), the largest of which may attain a length of over 4 metres, are particularly prized for their fatty meat. Lizard eggs are also eaten.

SNAKES (p : *snek, moran* (python);m : *gaigai*) Various

As with lizards, most species seem to be eaten, as are snake eggs. Snake meat is white and juicy, a little like eel though firmer. Sometimes large snakes are smoked and sections cut off as required; it is said the flavour improves with keeping.

INTRODUCED ANIMALS

Apart from cattle, goats, and a few guinea pigs and sheep (the latter introduced for their wool), two introduced animals are

136

136
Feeding a cassowary, Mendi, Southern Highlands Province

137 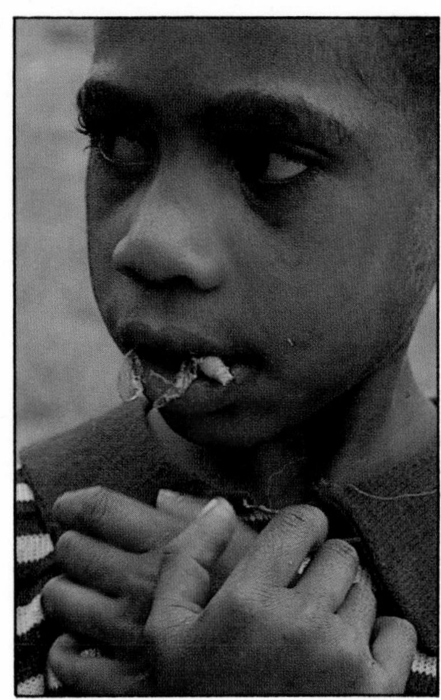

138 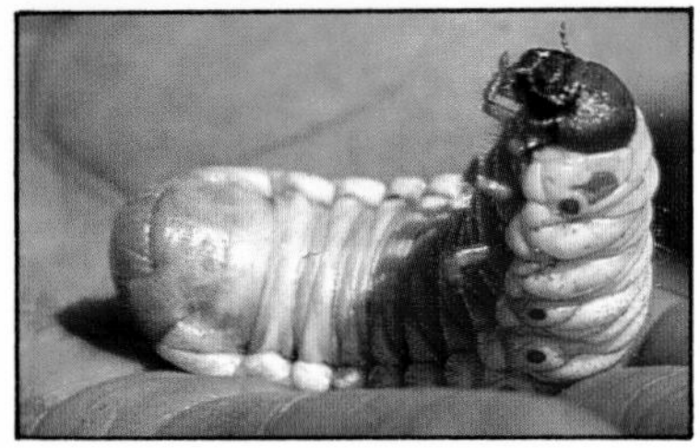

137
Boy eating a cicada, Markham Valley, Morobe Province

138
A giant tree grub, Western Province

139
Kaluli man eating sago grub, Southern Highlands Province

140
Sago grubs, Maprik, East Sepik Province

141
Nephila spiders, ready for eating

worth noting for their food potential; deer and buffalo. There are substantial numbers of introduced Rusa deer (*Cervus timorensis*) in the Morehead area of Western Province, and smaller populations of Rusa and Axis deer (*Axis axis*) in other places (including, it is said, the Port Moresby area). However, I have never seen venison on sale in Papua New Guinea. Buffalo steak has recently come on sale in Lae.

BIRDS (p : *pisin ;* m : *manu*) Various

Any bird, it would appear, has a reasonable chance of ending up on the Papua New Guinean table, though smaller birds have little to offer in the way of meat.

That which offers most as a table bird is the cassowary (p : *muruk ;* m : *kokokoko ; Casuarius* spp). A single bird may weigh around 30 kilograms. The cassowary is keenly hunted throughout its wide range, and in parts of the highlands, notably the Southern Highlands where it is important in trade and as a component of bride price payments, it is frequently semi-domesticated. There have been moves to establish commercial cassowary farming in the Southern Highlands. The feathers, bones and claws of the cassowary are also used for a variety of purposes including personal adornment, spear and arrow points, and lime spatulae.

The larger fruit-eating pigeons, and the crowned pigeons (*goura*) are also popular table birds. The Victoria Crowned Pigeon (*Goura victoria*), once common in northern Papua New Guinea, is said to be better meat than turkey; its flavour when cooked, is more exquisite by far than mutton, or oysters, or eggs. However, it is now a protected species. Other birds which are fairly important as food include the megapodes (scrub fowls and brush turkeys), ducks, geese, cockatoos, hornbills, larger parrots, and of course the domestic fowl. Before eating some of these, it may be worth recalling an old Australian bush recipe for cooking cockatoo : place the cockatoo and an old boot together in boiling water, cook until the boot is soft ; when it is, throw away the cockatoo and eat the boot.

While the eggs of most species may be eaten, a particular speciality are the eggs of the megapodes, which incubate their eggs either in mounds of soil and leaves, which generate heat through fermentation, or in sand that is heated by the sun or volcanic activity. In the Gazelle Pensinsula and in West New Britain there are large colonies of *Megapodius freycinet* and although the bird is protected, the large, reddish-brown eggs occasionally appear in Rabaul market. They have large yolks and are said to be rich in flavour.

FROGS

(p : *prok, rokrok* ; m : *parapara*) Various

Several species of frog and tadpole are used as food, particularly by children. Bulmer has recorded that among the Karam people of the Schrader Range in the Madang Province, all species except some toads and microhylid frogs are eaten, frequently bones and all. He also notes that leeches found in frogs are roasted, and considered a delicacy by women and girls.

139

OTHER THINGS THAT CREEP, CRAWL AND FLY

Numerous other small creatures are collected for eating, mostly by children, though their contribution to the overall food supply is marginal. Generally they are scorched and eaten as snacks, though sometimes they are cooked and added to grated tubers, or cooked in sago. A few are eaten raw.

140

The sago grub (Pidgin *binatang bilong saksak* ; *Rhyncosphorus ferringinlus papuanus*) is one of the better known delicacies. The grubs, a beetle larvae, are about 5 centimetres long, fat and cream in colour. In sago producing areas, palms are sometimes cut down in the knowledge that the grubs will breed in the rotting pith, and the grubs are 'harvested' after a couple of weeks. Usually the grubs are either boiled or roasted over an open fire. In the Maprik and Angoram (East Sepik) markets, and probably elsewhere, they are often sold spitted and grilled like *satay*. They are tender and very sweet with a slightly nutty flavour. The adult beetle is also eaten.

The larvae of a number of other insects, including beetles, butterflies, moths, wasps and dragonflies, are also eaten. Wasp nests are sometimes cut down onto open fires, providing an earth oven in which the larvae are baked. The adult of a hawk moth and another large unidentified moth, are scorched and eaten, or in the Sepik, wrapped in sago leaves and smoked, and several species of grasshopper, cricket, stick insect, cicada and beetle are consumed in various parts of the country, especially by children. Along the Sepik River, at least, mayflies are eaten when they appear briefly in large clouds; they are skimmed off the water when they fall and eaten raw or put into sago pancakes.

141

Another delicacy are the large orb weaving spiders (*Nephila* spp), which are plucked by the legs from their webs by the more intrepid, and lightly roasted over an open fire. Other spiders are also eaten, and Clarke records that the Bomagai-Angoiang (Maring) people of the central highlands eat a large hairy spider, which will bite when threatened; a case, it would seem, of biting the hand that it feeds.

142

STIMULANTS, SALT & EDIBLE EARTH

BETEL NUT (p : *buai* ; m : *buatau*) *Areca* spp.

Betel chewing is a national pastime ('*olsem bia bilong waitman*'). It is fairly widespread, though apparently only recently so in parts of the highlands, and is enjoyed by young and old.

The basic ingredient is the fruit of the areca palm, a small nut which is green when unripe, as it is usually eaten, and orange when ripe. The outer husk is stripped off - it is often chewed by small children - and the inside eaten. It is soft when unripe, but hardens. Areca palms (mostly *A. catechu*) are widely cultivated, but wild species (*A. jobiensis; A. macrocalyx*) often referred to in Pidgin as *kawiwi* or '*namba tu bilong buai*' are also collected. The fruit of another palm, *Ptychococcus paradoxus*, is also used.

The areca nut is usually eaten with lime (p : *kambang* ; m : *ahu*), which is found in natural deposits or processed from burnt coal or shells, or, with the leaves, catkin-like fruit or stems of the betel vine (p : *daka* ; m : *vaga*) *Piper betle*. In some parts of the country the mixture is prepared with a small wooden mortar and pestle by those whose teeth are no longer up to it.

Betel has a strongly astringent taste (due to tannins) and chewing it produces a red saliva, and brings about a general feeling of well being. The principal ingredient is an alkaloid, arecoline, which has properties similar to nicotine; it acts on the mucous membrane and on the central nervous system, lessening hunger and fatigue. Betel chewing also cleans your breath while it blackens your teeth.

Betel nut and lime play an important part in ceremonial life, and in traditional trade. Betel chewing is an essential part of any sort of celebration in most parts of the country and the nuts are frequently a component of bride price and other ritual exchanges. Lime is often used in magic, and lime containers (usually gourds or sections of bamboo) and spatulae (wood, turtleshell or bone) are often used to show status. Among some of the Sepik River people, lime spatulae used to be specifically decorated to indicate the number of homicides a man had accomplished.

 143

143
A happy *buai* eater, Tauri, East Sepik Province

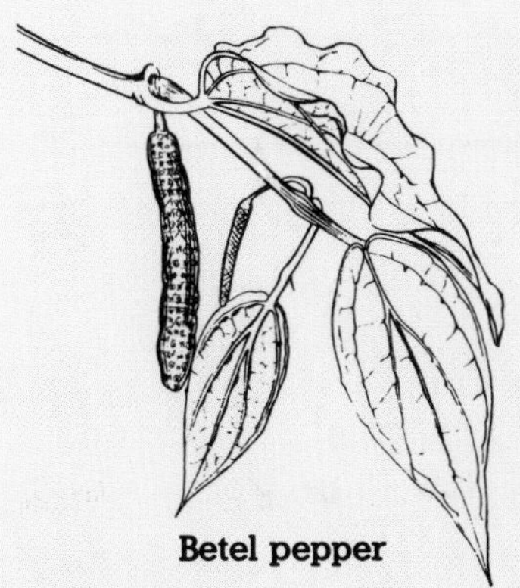

Betel pepper

TOBACCO (p : *brus* ; m : *kuku*) *Nicotiana tabacum*

Tobacco is a native of South America and was probably introduced to Papua New Guinea via Indonesia in the early

142
Gogodala man enjoying betel nut and lime, Western Province c1910

144

145

144
Kaluli man smoking tobacco pipe, Southern Highlands Province

145
House garden with tobacco plants and areca palms, Mambe, East Sepik Province

eighteenth century. It is now widespread, often growing right next to the house, and it is a common item of trade.

Tobacco is usually cured by hanging the leaves over the fire in a house. In some parts of the country the cured leaves are smoked through a bamboo pipe (p: *baubau;* m: *baubau*) which is closed at one end, the tobacco being placed in a small hole near the closed end. Otherwise, a cigarette is made by rolling the tobacco in leaves or newspaper. The *Post-Courier* claims to be the most widely smoked newspaper in the world.

Tobacco is grown commercially in the Eastern Highlands. As well as being used in the manufacture of cigarettes, a thick black twist tobacco is produced which is a popular item in village trade stores.

KAVA

Kava drinking, which is such an important part of social life in other parts of the Pacific, occurs (or until recently occurred) only in a few areas in the south of the Western Province and along the northern coast of the Huon Peninsula. Usually it was associated with ritual, particularly initiation and, in the Western Province, dugong and turtle hunting expeditions. Due to early mission and government opposition, the practice seems to be almost extinct, except amongst the Gogodala of the Aramia River area, where kava (*sika*) is still consumed. Kava (in the Kiwai language *gamada*) is an infusion of the crushed roots of the *Piper methysticum* plant. It is a mild narcotic.

146

147

146 147
Preparing *kava*, Western Province

TODDY

Unfortunately, toddy, which is a common beverage in other parts of the tropical world, is not widely made in Papua New Guinea, though it does occur in the Bamu River area of the Western Province and on the Polynesian outliers, Mortlock and Tasman islands.

Toddy is made from the sap of the coconut and other palms (including the sugar palm *Arenga saccharifera* and *Nypa fruticans*.)

The sap is collected from the young flower shoot, or spadix. The lower part of the spadix is tightly bound to prevent the flowers forming. The spadix is then cut off near the tip and the exposed tissues lightly cut. The sap which runs off is collected in a cup or section of bamboo. The spadix should be trained or weighted to hang down so that the sap does not run back down the spadix. A thin slice is taken off the spadix twice a day and after a day or so the sap begins to flow. Under expert tapping, a good palm may give juice for over two weeks, and may yield up to 4 litres a day at the peak flow. With village trees, about two pints seems a more reasonable expectation. Toddy may be drunk fresh or fermented; fermented toddy contains up to 8 per cent alcohol. In some parts of the world a spirit, arak, is distilled from fermented toddy. If fermentation is unchecked (it can be checked by adding a little lime to the container) the result is a clear vinegar. The toddy-collecting vessel should be kept covered. In some parts of the Pacific there is a beetle which has a propensity for falling into toddy; this usually kills the beetle but it also produces a corrosive irritant which may kill the drinker.

OTHER TRADITIONAL STIMULANTS

Reference has already been made (see p.83) to the consumption of certain mushrooms which are known to produce a state of aggression in some men and flirtation in some women, though it it not clear how much of this is psychologically induced and how much physiological.

Similar effects have been reported following the consumption of large quantities of steamed nuts of the *Castanopsis acuminatissima* and from eating a species of pandanus nut. In the case of pandanus, at least, this may be due to a mould.

Ginger is used as a stimulant and mangrove bark is sometimes used as a substitute for the areca nut. I was once shown a small green herb which was said to be *'olsem wiski'* - though I was at

148
Papua New Guinea tea and coffee

149
Coffee 'cherry'

150
Harvesting coffee, Goroka valley, Eastern Highlands Province

151
Tea picking, Mendi, Southern Highlands Province

148

the time too exhausted to take much interest. Straatmans's checklist also lists as stimulants, the leaves of *Callicarpa caudata, Cinnamomum* sp. (wild cinnamon), *Clerodendron paniculatum, Fleurya* sp. and *Phyllanthus* sp.; the juice of *Anamirta cocculus* and *Monstera* sp. (the fruit of the former, however, is poisonous), and the sap of the breadfruit tree.

149

COFFEE (p : *kopi* ; m : *kopi*) *Coffea* spp.

Coffee was introduced as a cash crop in Papua New Guinea in the 1920s. It is now the country's second largest export after copper.

There are two main species grown commercially: *C. arabica,* which grows at around 500 to 2000 metres, and *C. robusta* which grows below about 500 metres. Coffee drinkers generally prefer a blend of the rich *Arabica* and the more bitter *Robusta.* Papua New Guinea produces both, but is primarily a producer of *Arabica*, which was established in 1928 from cuttings of Jamaican Blue Mountain coffee (the coffee base of Tia Maria liqueur).

150

Ironically, it has, until quite recently, been difficult to buy a good roast coffee outside of the highlands and Lae. Most coffee packaged for local sale is pure Arabica and is often of indifferent quality. (Nunga is one of the more reliable brands and Korona dark roast is good if you can get it. People in Lae can usually get a pleasant blend of roasted coffee from the Namasu coffee factory). Worse, many of the country's leading hotels normally serve instant coffee imported from Australia.

TEA (p : *ti* ; m : *ti*) *Camellia sinensis*

151

Tea was introduced from Sarawak shortly before the Second World War, and established on a commercial basis after the War, from seed imported from Queensland and supplied to planters from a government plantation at Garaina in Morobe Province.

Papua New Guinea produces a fine, high quality tea. Several brands are fairly readily available, and all are good.

OTHER INFUSIONS

'Teas' may be made from a variety of other leaves, flowers or roots, fresh or dry. Try rosella, lemon grass, ginger, pawpaw flowers (all listed above) or hibiscus (*Hibiscus rosa-sinensis*) flowers.

For a change also try adding cardamom seeds to coffee and vanilla pods to tea. Both cardamom and vanilla are now grown in Papua New Guinea.

SALT (p: *sol;* m: *damena*)

Coastal people usually obtain salt by cooking their food in sea water, by evaporating sea water, or by burning driftwood or other substances which have been steeped in sea water. Sometimes seaweed encrusted with salt crystals is added to the cooking pot. Some inland people also obtain salt from the coast, either through trade or by making expeditions to the coast. In some parts of the country, inland people obtain salt from saline springs in much the same way as coastal people obtain it from sea water. Elsewhere, salt is obtained by burning certain plants (including banana fruit, coconut and *okari* nut husks, sago leaves, ferns, water-lily leaves, *pitpit* and Job's tears) and preparing from the ash, a saline solution which may then be evaporated. Vegetable salts usually consist primarily of potassium carbonate and potassium sulphate, as opposed to the predominant sodium chloride content of salt made from sea water and saline springs. The sodium content of some inland diets is very low.

152
Enga men at a saline spring

153
Salt-making, near Wonenara, Eastern Highlands Province

154
Slabs of salt made by the Anga at Wonenara, Eastern Highlands Province

Salt is an important item of traditional trade. In the eastern highlands the Anga (Kukukuku) people make a bitter pinkish-grey salt from *pitpit*, which is neatly packaged in bark-wrapped 'loaves' and smoked. It was once widely traded and can occasionally be found in the Lae market.

EDIBLE EARTH

In the East Sepik Province, people of the Pora Pora, Keram River and Marienburg hills areas eat a fine clay which is rich in kaolinite. Sometimes the clay is smoked over the fire, which gives a slight chocolatey flavour. Mostly the clay is eaten by pregnant women and children.

I have also been told of people eating a fine brown clay in a middle Sepik village, and in parts of Simbu Province an edible earth is believed to be a good tonic for pigs.

155 (*overleaf*)
Communal cooking, Trobriand Islands, c1919

152

153

154

PART TWO: CULINARY ARTS

156

PREPARATION AND EQUIPMENT

FOOD PREPARATION

For most foods bought in the market, preparation is fairly straightforward. However, in a few cases - and this applies more so with bush foods - some care is needed in handling and cooking. If not prepared correctly some plants can be poisonous. Also, several fruits and nuts which are edible when ripe are toxic when green and unripe. The fact that animals eat a plant does not necessarily mean it is fit for human consumption; on the other hand there are some, such as the *morinda*, which people say can only be eaten by pigs and cassowaries but which are, in fact, quite palatable (though only when completely ripe).

Poisons in plants are of three main types: cyanogenetic glucosides, which release prussic acid when crushed, alkaloids, and saponins. Some cyanogenetic glucosides give off a 'bitter almond' smell (benzaldehyde) and some alkaloids and saponins are very bitter. The presence of saponins may be indicated if, when the crushed plant is shaken up in water, a froth appears and remains for some time.

Most harmful substances can be removed by thorough washing, which is more effective if the plant is grated first, or by cooking. (However, for reasons given below, do *not* wash taro). Usually two or three hours in water is sufficient but with some plants, such as *Cycas circinalis* seeds and *Pangium edule* seeds, a longer period is advisable; in parts of the Eastern Highlands *Pangium* seeds are first cooked and then left for three months in running water. (Soaking in water is also an effective way of dealing with 'overripe' meat.)

Among the more common vegetables, taro should be treated with a little respect by those not familiar with it. Some taros (see p.46) contain saponins and should be thoroughly cooked. Also, both the leaves and tubers of a large number of taros contain calcium oxalate crystals which 'fight the mouth' if not removed by thorough cooking and can also cause irritation to the hands if peeled under water. If you do get caught, lime juice will ease the irritation. Some species of yam (see p.48) contain a bitter alkaloid, dioscorine, which is poisonous and must be removed by thorough washing, by cooking, or by the addition of lime juice to the cooking water. Tapioca (cassava, manioc) tubers, especially those which have a bitter taste, may contain a cyanogenetic glucoside, and should be grated and washed before cooking. The Polynesian arrowroot also requires thor-

156
Preparing *mon*, Malasiga village, Morobe Province; adding coconut milk (see p.118)

ough cooking. Wild hyacinth and lima bean - and probably other wild beans - can be poisonous.

Cycas circinalis has already been mentioned as a potentially poisonous plant (this goes for the edible fronds as well as the fruit) as has *Pangium edule*. Other less common fruits and nuts listed in chapter three which are edible but should be treated respectfully are *Aleurites moluccana* (the candlenut), gourds and related plants, *Passiflora foetida* (a wild passionfruit) and species of *Albizia, Barringtonia, Sterculia* and *Tephrosia.*

Caution should also be exercised in eating fungi, though most people are already excessively cautious about fungi, most of which are edible.

EQUIPMENT

The recipes set out in chapter six have been framed on the assumption that the average reader will normally be using a 'European'-style kitchen. However, I would strongly urge anyone living in Papua New Guinea to cook, at least occasionally, over an open fire in a traditional clay pot. The Adzera pots of the Markham valley are as easily available as any and are excellent cooking pots. Motu pots and occasionally pots from Wanigela and the Amphlett Islands are obtainable in Port Moresby and Lae and are also good. Some foods, such as baked fish, yam pudding and *ubai* (see recipes), are best when cooked over an open fire, wrapped in banana, ginger or betel vine leaves (or aluminium foil). The more enthusiastic will also construct a *mumu* pit (see p. 32); this calls for a spade, a stout back, a quantity of evenly-sized round river stones, and a good supply of wood.

Essential cooking equipment is a coconut scraper, which traditionally consists of a serrated blade mounted on a low stool. Beautifully sculptured traditional graters from the Mortlock Islands (locally *te tuai*) are sometimes available from artifact shops; otherwise, at the time of writing, very good metal blades were being produced by the St Josephs Vocational Training Centre just outside Lae. More sophisticated imported graters are becoming available but they have little to offer over the traditional grater. For grating coconut you will also need a reasonably large bowl. The canoe-shaped wooden bowls of the Tami Islands (traditionally used for taro) are excellent for this, as are the large round wooden bowls of the Rai coast and some of the round wooden bowls from the Trobriand Islands and other parts of Milne Bay. For cutting coconuts you may need a Chinese chopper, a meat axe or a sharp bush knife. If you cook in coconut shells you will need a hacksaw. For cooking soups (and for making fresh fruit juice) a large electric blender is a useful piece of equipment. Alternatively you will need an efficient food mill or a large, strong strainer and a good deal of patience.

Papua New Guinea's traditional cooks specialize in what might be called plain cooking. To use local foods in a more varied menu, imagination is necessary. Especially with sensible substitution, inspiration may be gleaned from Chinese, southeast Asian and Indian recipes; otherwise, of a number of tropical cookbooks I have seen the only ones I would recommend with any enthusiasm are *A Taste of the Tropics*, by Susan Parkinson and Peggy Stacy (Mills and Boon, London, 1972) *The Cooking of the Caribbean Islands*, by Linda Wolfe, in the Time-Life Foods of the World series (1970, 1971), and *Cooking with Exotic Fruit*, by Selma and W.J.A. Payne (Batsford, London, 1979.)

SOME PRELIMINARIES

157
Preparing coconut milk, Bilbil, Madang Province

USING COCONUTS

Coconuts can be enjoyed in a number of ways and are an essential ingredient in Papua New Guinea cooking.

For drinking, use green coconuts, chilled if possible.

To make coconut milk, take a mature nut (shake to make sure there is water inside): break into halves, saving the water in a bowl, and scrape both halves on a coconut scraper into the bowl. Let it sit for a few minutes then squeeze the liquid from the grated flesh through a strainer. This will give a fairly rich milk. Some people prefer to add water before squeezing. As well as being excellent as a base for boiling vegetables and for use in many southeast Asian recipes, coconut milk can be used to make some delicious soups and drinks (see below). Especially in those parts of the country subject to early Polynesian missionary influence, coconut milk is often used as a substitute for cow's milk in non-traditional recipes. Scones made with coconut milk are delicious, though I am not so fond of coconut milk in coffee. When cooking with coconut milk, avoid boiling; coconut milk will curdle.

If coconut milk is left in a cool place for a few hours, a thick cream will rise to the top (note, however, that the milk ferments fairly easily). This cream may be used like dairy cream, and if churned, will yield a sweet white butter.

Coconut oil is obtained by briskly cooking coconut milk for a couple of hours. The clear oil will rise to the top and can be poured off.

The flesh of the mature nut, cut straight from the shell or grated and roasted is pleasant as a snack and as an accompaniment to curry. Grated coconut also has countless uses in making desserts and sweets.

COOKING ROOTS AND TUBERS

Traditionally, roots and tubers are usually boiled, steamed or baked. Very broadly, they can be used in much the same way as the potato. The more common tubers (and also plantains and breadfruit) all make good chips if sliced thinly, and in the case of taro and yams, washed to remove excess starch. Mashed sweet potato is pleasant, especially if liberally buttered. Baked sweet potato is a must with roast dinners. *Hasbin* tubers are delicious cooked, like new potatoes, with butter and parsley, or a fresh green such as *Oenanthe javanica*. Sweet potato, taro and yam all make good bases for soups, especially if you use a blender. Southern United States recipes for 'yams' (as sweet potatoes are called there) suggest some interesting ways of cooking *kaukau* (see p.153). From taro and yams you can make a paste which can be used in much the same way as pastry (for example see pp. 152-159).

USING SAGO

Most Europeans think of sago in a granulated form as an ingredient in puddings. Traditional methods of cooking sago are summarized in chapter three (pp.54-55). A little sago flour is a good thickener for soups; mix in a little cold water first and slowly add hot liquids to it. Sago makes a good 'wrapping' for other foods; sago pancakes wrapped around tinned meat or fish and greens, or such exotica as mayflies, makes a good meal when you are hungry. Sago mixed with banana, coconut or breadfruit makes good dumplings.

JUICES AND SYRUPS

Fresh juice and syrups can be made from just about any local fruit (though you would not think so if you looked at the amount this country spends each year on imported fruit juice!). With a blender, simply slice fruit into reasonable sized pieces, peeling fruit if necessary, and add water and sugar. The proportions of fruit, water and sugar depend on the fruit and on personal tastes. For syrups, use more sugar and boil until the liquid is sufficiently concentrated. Fivecorners make a particularly good fruit juice; I use three medium size fruit and about 50 grams of sugar to a litre of water.

USING PAWPAW

Pawpaw is usually eaten ripe as a fruit. Eaten green, it is a pleasant vegetable, a little like pumpkin. Pawpaw contains an enzyme, papain, which is a very effective meat tenderizer and thus may be a useful addition to stews and beef curries. The not-quite-ripe fruit is also pleasant fried as a vegetable.

HERBS

In traditional cooking, greens serve partly as a vegetable and partly as a flavouring, but flavourings in general do not have the importance in Papua New Guinea cooking that they do in European, American and Asian cooking. Several, however, are good substitutes for European herbs. *Oenanthe javanica* is a good substitute for parsley or dill and *Rungia klossii* is a reasonable substitute for basil, though neither is particularly close in flavour. Other greens which are useful either as flavourings or as fresh salad vegetables are *Commelina*, cress, watercress, pigweed, *Coleus* and *Euodia*. There are probably others.

JAMS, JELLIES, CHUTNEYS AND PICKLES

Many of the fruit available in Papua New Guinea yield excellent jams, jellies, chutneys or pickles.

As a general principle, for jam-making first cook the fruit - which should not be too ripe - in about half its volume of water till it is soft. If fruit is low on acid (as are, for example, guava, passionfruit and pawpaw) add a little lime juice. Then combine equal volumes of fruit pulp and sugar and boil till the sugar dissolves. Remove any froth which forms on the surface during cooking. The pectin in the fruit will ensure that it sets. To test if it is ready, place a little on a saucer and see if it forms a skin. When it is set, the hot jam should be poured into sterile jars which are then carefully sealed. The methods of cooking jam and jelly are essentially the same, but in the case of jelly the cooked fruit should be put through a fine strainer (or double thickness cheese cloth, butter muslin or mosquito netting) before adding the sugar.

Among the local fruits which make good jams are mango, pineapple, pawpaw, guava, rosella, banana, rose apple, soursop, Polynesian plum, tree tomato, passionfruit, granadilla (the flesh as well as the seeds), *garcinia*, Jamaica Cherry, Indian plum and wild berries.

An interesting honey substitute can be made by boiling the skins and cores of pineapple and then cooking the strained liquid with an equal volume of sugar.

In Asia people often make fresh chutneys, using fresh fruit, spices (almost always including chilli), salt and sometimes a little lime juice. These are made about an hour or two before the meal but do not keep. One interesting chutney is made by blending fresh coriander leaves, grated coconut, onions, ginger, chilli, salt, pepper, a little sugar, and lime juice and water. Preserved chutneys and pickles are usually cooked in vinegar. Green mangoes are perhaps the most widely used fruit in chutney making but other fruits worth trying are pineapple, choko, pawpaw, guava, rose apple, Polynesian plum, cucumber and coconut.

For a basic sweet mango chutney: peel and slice a dozen green mangoes and parboil about 8 cm of fresh ginger root; next boil 500ml malt vinegar and 1 kg of sugar until the sugar is dissolved (about 5 minutes); add to this the mangoes, finely sliced ginger, 6 ground birdseye chillies, 1 sliced onion, pepper, a handful of raisins and perhaps some *galip* nuts; cook slowly till you have a thick chutney (about 30 minutes) and then bottle.

THE MENU

Traditionally meals were a one course affair (though often this was a combination of soup and solids), with snacks in between meals. But even the most ardent supporters of the 'Melanesian way' no longer seem to regard this traditional as a constraint on eating, and indeed, with a little imagination it is not difficult to plan an interesting 6 course meal using predominantly local ingredients. Friends in Port Moresby, irritated by a neighbour's complaints about the food available in Port Moresby, invited the neighbour to dinner with the following menu (though this did take a little organization):

---

boiled crab

whole barramundi and bass baked in banana leaves

barbecued wild duck with lime sauce

venison cooked *mumu* style with taro, sweet potato, *aibika* and water *kaukau*

frozen pineapple dessert

Some people seem to regard soups as unsuitable to a hot climate but we find ourselves eating a lot of soup - hot as well as chilled. Soups are easy to prepare (especially with a blender), easy to eat, and are a good way of using local vegetables and greens if you find traditional cooking methods a little dull.

Perhaps it is as well for the local fauna, but it is remarkable (compared to say, New Caledonia) how little advantage the expatriate population takes of local seafood and meat other than beef and pork. People - especially the expatriate population - could also take much more advantage than they do of local vegetables, particularly greens. Not only are they tasty, they are generally much less expensive and frequently more nutritious than imported vegetables.

In the recipes which follow I have not distinguished between entrees and main courses (many of the recipes could be either), but some of the foods which you might think about using in interesting entrees are crab, shellfish, smoked fish, sea urchin, *pitpit*, and avocado.

It is surprising also, how seldom people serve fresh local fruit at the end of a meal or use local fruit in drinks. Many dinner guests are pleased to be introduced to even such relatively common fruit and nuts as custard apple, soursop, tree tomato, *laulau*, cashew nut fruit, Jamaica cherry, *okari* and *galip*. For a real novelty, serve *morinda* (Indian mulberry) fruit at the end of a meal - as a substitute for cheese.

I do not intend to give a list of possible menus, but as an example of what might be done with local foods here are three menu suggestions from the recipes given below.

Mock melokhia soup

Potted fish
served with SP lager

Chicken in *galip* sauce
Tapioca balls
Hasbin salad
served with more SP lager

Bananas flambe

Chilled watercress soup

Pitpit with Hollandaise sauce
served with dry white wine

Fish Kokoda

Barramundi in red wine sauce
Creamed breadfruit
served with dry red wine

Fresh fruit

Turtle Soup
served with dry sherry

Crab Creole
served with champagne

Pork *marita*
Boiled highland potatoes
Fried greens
served with burgundy

Mango sherbet

CHAPTER SIX

RECIPES

Unless otherwise indicated, the quantities given in these recipes are adequate for six servings.

All measurements are metric. To convert from centigrade to Fahrenheit oven temperatures use the following rough equivalents:

°C	°F
150	300
175	350
225	450

PUMPKIN SOUP

1 medium sized pumpkin (1-1½kg)
1½ litres chicken stock
100g butter
milk of one coconut
1 teaspoon of coriander
salt, pepper.

Peel the pumpkin, remove the seeds and cut into slices for easy cooking. Boil in the chicken stock and butter, adding coriander, salt and pepper. When the pumpkin is cooked (about 30 minutes) put the lot in a blender. Return to the saucepan and add the coconut milk. Reheat but do not boil.

If possible garnish with fresh basil.

This soup may be eaten hot or cold.

An alternative method is to serve the soup, chilled, in the pumpkin shell. In this case do not peel the pumpkin but carefully scape out the raw flesh.

BREADFRUIT SOUP

Take a ripe breadfruit. Puncture the skin and bake the fruit for about an hour in a 175° oven. When it is cool enough to handle, remove the flesh from the skin, separating out any seeds. Add this to about a litre of heated chicken stock, season with salt, pepper and coriander and add the lime juice. Combine these ingredients in a blender (or else push the breadfruit flesh through a strainer and mix well) and reheat till not quite boiling. Before serving stir in the cream and sherry. If you have it, garnish with fresh basil, mint or *Oenanthe javanica.*

This is a very rich soup. It may be served hot or cold.

1 breadfruit (about 1kg)
1 litre chicken stock
juice of one lime
1 teaspoon coriander
salt, pepper
200ml cream
100ml sherry (optional)

GREENS AND COCONUT SOUP

1 bunch of leafy greens
2 medium sized potatoes or 1 medium sized taro (about 500g)
1 litre chicken or beef stock
milk of 1 coconut
salt, pepper

Boil the potatoes or taro (which are there for texture) in the stock for about 20 minutes. (If you do not have fresh stock use one stock cube to half a litre of water). Add the greens, salt and pepper and cook for a further 10 minutes. Just about any green will do; my own preferences are amaranth, water *kaukau*, fern leaf, and pumpkin shoots. Put the mixture through a blender. If you use pumpkin shoots it is also a good idea to put the mixture through a coarse strainer. Add the coconut milk and reheat but do not boil.

MON (PAWPAW SOUP)

2 litres water
salt
about 250g sago (or 2 tablespoons cornflour)
1 medium to large pawpaw
4 or 5 small chillies (birdseye chillies)
cream of 1 coconut.

Mix the sago with a little salted cold water then add hot water. Traditionally *mon* has a very gluggy consistency; expatriates may prefer to use less sago (or cornflour) to obtain a soup of more familiar consistency. Peel and slice a ripe pawpaw and add it to the sago, together with the chopped chillies, stirring continuously. When the pawpaw is fully integrated, add the coconut cream, reheat (but do not boil) and serve.

From Malasiga village, Morobe Province

SOUP-ON-PATROL

water
leafy greens
soy sauce
sesame oil
egg (optional)

For those who spend some time in the bush, and who have a finite appetite for starchy staples, three commodities which are easily carried and can greatly enhance the quality of life, are tabasco, soy sauce and sesame oil.

The following recipe is a useful one on patrol: it is nutritious, easy to digest after a long walk, and requires little effort to prepare.

Boil the water and add soy sauce to flavour, and a dash of sesame oil (which is available in quite small bottles). Add a handful or two of any greens which are available (or spring onions) and let them cook for about 2 minutes. If you have an egg you can drop this in at the last moment and stir.

TOMATO, CRAB AND CARDAMOM SOUP

Australia's greatest contribution to world cuisine is not the pavlova; it is Rosella tomato soup. You may make your own tomato soup base if you wish but I recommend Rosella.

Cook the crab and remove the meat. Meanwhile boil the potatoes in the water, and when boiled reduce them and the water to a puree. To this puree add the tomato soup from the tin and a tinful of milk. Mix thoroughly and heat together with the crab meat, crushed cardamom seeds (which are grown in Papua New Guinea), salt and pepper until just below boiling point.

2 tins Rosella tomato soup
1 tin milk
1½ tins water
2 medium sized potatoes (about 500g)
2 medium sized crabs
cardamom seeds (about 5 pods)
salt, pepper

MOCK MELOKHIA

When I first began experimenting with local greens I found that *aibika* (*Hibiscus manihot*), while pleasant in flavour, was too gelatinous to eat on its own as a vegetable. Hence the idea of mock melokhia. Melokhia has been, for a long time, a staple of the Egyptian peasant. The leaves of melokhia (*Corchorus olitorius*) are added to whatever stock is available; the leaves provide the texture of the soup but its distinctive flavour comes from a paste made from garlic, coriander and pepper. The two varieties of *aibika* (or *aibika* and *aupa*) give an excellent rendition of melokhia; indeed I think they are an improvement on it.

1 bunch each of *aibika* and *aupa*
1½ litres of chicken stock
3 cloves garlic, crushed
2 teaspoons ground coriander
a dash of cayenne pepper
10g butter (or 1 tablespoon oil)

Take roughly equal portions of *aibika* (*H. manihot*) and *aupa* (Amaranth); a 20 toea bunch of each is sufficient for about 1½ litres of stock. Remove the coarser stalks and chop until you have almost a puree (that is most of the work). Boil about 1½ litres of chicken stock. When the water boils add the greens. Meanwhile heat the butter in a frying pan and when that is hot, prepare a paste with garlic, coriander and cayenne pepper; add this to the soup. The leaves should boil for about 3 minutes. The timing of this is important; if they cook for too short a time the leaves will float on top; if they cook for too long they will sink to the bottom and a horrible green foam will appear.

CUCUMBER SOUP

The brown and yellow cucumbers which are especially common in Koki market are a bit too dry and bitter to make a good salad vegetable, but they make excellent cucumber soup.

6 medium sized cucumbers (in total about 2½kg)
1 large potato (about 400g)
1 litre chicken stock
salt, pepper
250ml cream
dill (for garnish)

Cook the cucumbers and potato in the seasoned stock for about 30 minutes then put through a blender. Stir in the cream and garnish with dill.

This soup is best served cold.

CLAM CHOWDER

250g shellfish
2 rashers bacon
3 medium onions (total about 300g)
2 large potatoes (total about 800g)
½ litre water
½ litre milk
50g butter
salt, pepper

Large clam-like bivalves (*Geloina coaxans*) are often on sale in Koki and Gordons markets, and small clam-like bivalves (*Atactodea striata* - see p.84) may be gathered along the tidemark of most white sand beaches along the Papuan coastline. Both make good clam chowder but any other shellfish will do.

Wash the shellfish carefully, steam open and remove the meat. Dice the onions and potatoes and cook them, together with the butter, salt and pepper, in the water. Meanwhile slice the bacon, fry it till brown and add to the onions and potatoes. When the onions and potatoes are cooked, (after about 15 minutes) add the shellfish and milk and bring to just below boiling point.

New England recipe

FISH SOUP

Fish stock can be easily prepared from the heads, tails and bones of fish; it provides a useful base for soups.

Boil the stock together with the sliced potato, yam or taro (which gives the soup texture), onion and salt and pepper (or cayenne) for about 30 minutes. Add the lemon juice and coconut milk and reheat without boiling. Pieces of fish may also be added.

A variation on this is to use chicken or fish stock and add the meat from 1 large crab.

Garnish with parsley.

1 litre fish stock
2 medium sized potatoes or 1 medium sized yam or taro - (about 500g)
1 onion
milk of 1 coconut
squeeze of lime juice
salt and pepper

BECHE-DE-MER SOUP

10 bêche-de-mer
1 litre water
2 slices onion
salt, pepper
parsley (for garnish)

Gather the small black bêche-de-mer which are common along most of the Papua New Guinea coastline. Cut them across the middle and squeeze, 'when a small skein of ova will come away'. The ova should be white, cream or pale pink; if they are orange or red, discard them.

Wash the ova and place in a saucepan with the water, onion, salt and pepper. Cook for about 30 minutes and strain (some people prefer to leave the ova in the soup). Garnish with chopped parsley.

As well as obtaining a delicately flavoured clear soup, you may help remove some people's reservations about swimming in places like Ela beach.

From *South Sea Island Recipes* (Suva, 1934), recipe by Mrs Willoughby Tottenham.

TURTLE SOUP

½kg of turtle meat (preferably not too fatty, and with a bit of skin - to assist the soup to gel)
2 litres of water
salt and pepper
150ml sherry or madeira (optional)

There are many more elaborate recipes for turtle soup (the Wine and Food Society's *Guide to Soups* refers to 'that triumph of cooking, turtle soup') but this one has the advantage of simplicity.

Cut the turtle meat into smallish pieces and cook in the water simmering for about two to three hours. Then strain the liquid, add salt and pepper (a little cayenne is perhaps best) and a few shreds of meat and reheat till the soup begins to gel. Either serve it hot (with the addition - optional - of a glassful of sherry or madeira just before serving) or as a cold consomme. A slice of lime makes a nice garnish.

This recipe may also be used as a basic stock to which may be added vegetables and other seasoning.

PAUA SUP

This recipe, kindly supplied by Mr Joe Chan of Port Moresby, is a traditional Papua New Guinea Chinese recipe. It is included for interest, since the major ingredient, pythons, are protected species. (The reader may, however, care to try the flying fox varient.)

First catch your snake. By tradition this should be either the amethystine python (*Liasis amethystinus*) or the olive python (*Bothrochilus papuanus*). The snake is then tied to a pole, and, *while still alive*, skinned and all excess fat removed. The gall bladder is also removed; it may be kept and put to other culinary-medicinal uses. The snake is then chopped into lengths of about 10cm and placed into cold water which is brought to the boil and allowed to simmer for 3 to 4 hours. (The head of the snake may be kept separately. If it is boiled in water, the liquid is said to be useful as a remedy against choking.) When cooking is complete, the water is thrown away and the snake flesh retained.

Meanwhile, a stock is prepared separately from chicken ('an *old* chook') and/or pork scraps. While this is cooking (also 3 to 4 hours) the fat is periodically skimmed off the top and discarded. After cooking, when the stock has cooled, all flesh is removed from the bones and retained, and the extraneous elements thrown away.

Also at the same time, a 'herb soup' is prepared in another pot. Various green herbs may be used, but the principle 'herb' is *yatchoi* (preserved cabbage?). Some cooks also use large quantities of ginger.

When the chicken/pork stock and the herb soup have cooled, these and the snake flesh are all combined. Bean noodles (*funsi*) are added and the soup again brought to the boil. As an optional extra, brandy may be added.

The whole operation is said to take 6 to 7 hours (exclusive of catching the snake).

I have not eaten *paua sup*, but I am reliably informed that it causes the consumer to perspire (an effect of the ginger and brandy, perhaps, rather than the python) and to experience a powerful feeling of healthiness.

Paua sup may also be made from flying fox. The basic recipe is the same (with special emphasis on removing all fat), except that sugar cane is added to the stock.

WATERCRESS SOUP

1 bunch of watercress
1 litre of chicken or beef stock
2 medium sized potatoes (about 500g)
salt, pepper
250ml cream

Boil the potato in the seasoned stock for about 20 minutes then add the watercress with most of the stalks removed. Cook for a further ten minutes and then put the mixture through a blender. Stir in the cream and reheat but do not boil. Garnish with fresh watercress leaves.

TSALINGU

yams
water
coconut cream
salt

Slice the yams and cook in water with a little salt until you have a thick soup (proportions of yam to water seem to vary a good deal.) Add coconut cream and serve.

Traditional Abelam recipe

BAKED CRAB CREOLE

- 6 large crabs (or two 170g tins of crab meat)
- 50g fresh white bread crumbs
- 3 tablespoons annatto flavoured oil
- 3 cloves garlic
- 50g peppers (preferably the mildly hot variety)
- 100ml sherry
- juice of two limes
- a few sprigs of parsley
- liberal pinch of cayenne
- salt, pepper
- butter
- 2 tablespoons grated parmesan cheese

Boil the crabs and remove the meat, making sure to avoid all the shell and cartilage. Add the breadcrumbs and mix thoroughly into the shredded crabmeat.

In a frying pan, heat the annatto flavoured oil (this is prepared by steeping bixa seeds in a little vegetable oil - see p.83. If you cannot find bixa you may substitute mace). Cook the crushed garlic and finely chopped peppers, stirring constantly, until they are soft but not brown (about 5 minutes). Then add the sherry, lime juice, parsley, cayenne, salt and pepper. Mix these well then add the crab and breadcrumbs. When thoroughly integrated, transfer to a 20cm pie dish, sprinkle the parmesan cheese over the top and dot with butter.

Bake at 150° for about 30 minutes or until the cheese is brown.

These quantities should be adequate for an entree for 6 people.

Caribbean recipe.

FISH KOKODA

500g raw fish
250ml lime juice
2 tablespoons finely chopped onion (optional)
3 birdseye chillies (or ¼ teaspoon tabasco)
250ml coconut milk
salt

Fillet the fish and cut into thin strips. Marinade it in the lime juice, onion, chopped chilli, and salt for about 2 hours. The flesh will turn white, as though cooked. About 10 minutes before serving add the coconut cream.

Some people prefer to discard the marinade before adding the coconut milk, perhaps adding a little fresh lime juice at the same time.

If limes are not available the same effect can be achieved by squeezing on the fish, the juices of 4 or 5 hermit crabs.

Green prawns and fresh shellfish may be substituted for the raw fish.

SAGO-COCONUT PANCAKES WITH PRAWN FILLING

To make the pancakes, mix the 'batter' of sago flour and coconut, moistening if necessary with water or coconut milk (the mixture does not have to be as moist as a normal pancake batter). Heat a little butter and cook the pancake (allowing about 10 minutes for each side).

For the filling, make a white sauce from the butter, flour, milk, salt and pepper (see p.136) and the paprika. Shell, devein, and chop the prawns and cook them till pink then add to the white sauce.

Fill the pancakes with the mixture and serve.

1 cup sago flour
1 cup grated coconut
butter
salt

FILLING
1 cup (about 250g) prawns
50g butter
1 tablespoon cornflour
500ml milk (or coconut milk)
1 tablespoon paprika
salt, pepper

BARRAMUNDI IN RED WINE SAUCE

1kg barramundi
flour
3 tablespoons olive oil

RED WINE SAUCE:
1 medium sized onion (100g)
3 cloves garlic
2 tablespoons flour
2 tablespoons olive oil
500ml red wine
500ml water
1 tablespoon tomato paste
1 bay leaf
thyme
parsley
1 teaspoon capers

This recipe is based on a Provencal dish. The sauce, in Provence *raito*, is said to have been brought to ancient Marseille by the Phoenicians. In Provence the sauce is frequently served with whiting, but it goes well with local barramundi.

To prepare the sauce : heat the olive oil and add the onion and garlic ; cook till the onion begins to brown. Add the flour and stir in carefully. Add the red wine and boiling water and bring the mixture to the boil. Add the tomato paste and herbs (but not the capers) and cook until the sauce thickens (about 10 minutes); by this time the sauce will have reduced to about a third of its original volume. Put it through a strainer and keep hot.

Cut the barramundi into bite size slices, roll in the flour, then put in hot olive oil and cook quickly (about 10 minutes.) When cooked, remove the fish from the pan, add to the red wine sauce and cook for a further 10 minutes or so. Add the capers just before serving.

PSARI PLAKI

This Mediterranean dish is an especially good recipe for cooking fish whose flesh is too coarse or flavour too strong or too oily for successful grilling or baking.

Heat the chopped onion and garlic in some of the oil until lightly browned. Add the tomatoes, greens, a liberal amount of parsley, dill, salt, pepper and white wine, and cook for a further 15 minutes.

Clean the fish, cut into bite size pieces and place in a heavy pan with the rest of the oil and the juice of half the lemon or lime. When the tomato mixture is cooked, pour this over the fish and add the other half of lemon or lime, sliced thinly. Cover and cook on a low heat for about 30 to 40 minutes (depending on the fish). A couple of handfuls of black olives can be added about 10 minutes before the cooking is finished.

1½kg fish
150ml olive oil
3 medium sized onions (total about 300g)
4 cloves garlic
6 medium sized tomatoes (or two 425g tins)
250g fresh silver beet or water *kaukau*
parsley (optional)
dill (or mint)
150ml white wine
1 lemon or lime
salt, pepper
black olives (optional)

Greek recipe

PRAWN CREOLE

1kg prawns (uncooked)
3 tablespoons annatto flavoured oil
1 medium sized onion
5 or 6 birdseye chillies
1 tablespoon plain flour
6 medium sized tomatoes (or two 425g tins)
1 tablespoon tomato paste
2 bay leaves
a few sprigs of parsley
salt, pepper

Shell and devein the prawns.

In a frying pan, heat the annatto flavoured oil (see p.83). When the oil is hot, add the finely chopped onion and chillies and cook, stirring frequently, until the onion is soft (about 5 minutes). Add the flour and stir until a paste begins to form. Next add the finely sliced tomatoes, tomato paste, bay leaf, chopped parsley, salt and pepper and cook uncovered until most of the liquid has evaporated. Finally, add the prawns and cook on a low heat until the prawns turn pink (this will take 2 to 3 minutes).

Serve with rice.

GARLIC PRAWNS

500g prawns (shelled)
125g butter
6 cloves garlic
a sprig of parsley
2 tablespoons of chopped spring onions
salt, pepper

Shell and devein the prawns.

Melt a third of the butter in a pan. Add the garlic, crushed, and saute the prawns for about 2 minutes. Season with salt and pepper. Add the rest of the butter to melt as a sauce. Scatter the chopped onion and parsley in the pan. Serve immediately, on a bed of plain or saffron rice.

(These quantities should be adequate for an entree for six people.)

BAKED FISH WITH LEMON GRASS

Fish
lemon grass
soy sauce (optional)
ginger or banana leaves or aluminium foil (for cooking)

Gut and clean the fish (any fish) and fill the stomach cavity with bruised lemon grass. If you like, moisten the outside of the fish with a little soy sauce. Wrap in ginger and banana leaves (or aluminium foil) and cook in the ashes of a fire. A fish of about 1-2kg will normally take about 30 minutes in good hot ashes.

On using banana leaf wrapping:
Remove the pithy stem which runs down the centre of the leaf and heat the leaf gently over a fire; this softens the leaf so that it can be folded without splitting and the pith can be used for tying.

SCRAMBLED TURTLE EGGS

10 turtle eggs
300ml milk (or coconut milk)
25g butter (or a little oil)
salt, pepper

Turtle eggs are tasty but they have the disconcerting trait that the 'whites' do not turn solid and white on cooking as most eggs do. Hence it is best to eat them scrambled (or, of course, raw).

Mix the eggs, milk, salt and pepper in a bowl. Heat the butter in a pan and when it is hot add the seasoned eggs and milk. Stir continually. The mixture is inclined to be a little watery at first but becomes crisp.

For added nourishment, add finely chopped greens to the mixture.

FISH CAKES AND ANCHOVY SAUCE

500g cooked fish
500g sweet potato
1 egg
salt, pepper
flour
vegetable oil

ANCHOVY SAUCE:
50g butter
1 tablespoon cornflour
500ml milk
salt, pepper
4 anchovies
1 teaspoon tinned fish paste or ¼ teaspoon shrimp paste (blachan) (optional)

Boil the sweet potato and combine with the finely shredded cooked fish, egg, salt and pepper. Form into flat cakes, roll in flour and fry in hot oil.

Make a white sauce with the butter, flour, milk, salt and pepper (see p.136) and add the ground-up anchovies. The optional addition of fish paste or blachan gives additional flavour and colour.

SEA URCHIN OMELETTE

Collect the sea urchins, being careful not to get pricked by the spines (which can be mildly poisonous). Break open the sea urchin and remove the five orange or pink ovaries, or coral, from the centre. Discard the rest.

Break the eggs into a bowl and add the water salt and pepper. Beat with a fork for a minute or so and then add the sea urchin corals.

Heat the butter and add the mixture. Cook for about 3 minutes, turn and cook for another minute or so (as for any omelette).

This makes one omelette, enough for one person.

15 sea urchins
3 eggs
2 tablespoons water
salt, pepper
50g butter (or 2 tablespoons oil)

POTTED FISH

Steam the fish and carefully remove all bones and skin. Meanwhile melt the butter.

Mash the fish into a fine pulp and add the blue cheese, most of the melted butter (a little at a time), Worcestershire sauce, salt and pepper. Mix the lot until you have a creamy paste. Place this in a deepish dish and seal with the rest of the butter.

Serve on toast as an entree. Potted fish will keep well until the seal is broken but should not be kept more than a day or two after.

500g smoked fish (smoked *tilapia* is good)
250g butter
100g blue cheese
1 tablespoon Worcestershire sauce
salt, pepper

FISH, LOBSTER AND CRAB MORNAY

500g cooked fish, lobster and crab-meat

WHITE SAUCE:
50g butter
1 tablespoon cornflour
500ml milk
parsley
salt, pepper
100g grated cheese
6-12 mushrooms (optional)

To prepare the white sauce: melt the butter on a low heat, and when melted add the cornflour, stirring carefully to avoid lumps. When the flour and butter form a smooth paste, slowly add the milk. Finally add parsley, salt and pepper.

Meanwhile, lightly cook the sliced mushrooms in a little butter and set aside.

Add the fish, lobster and crabmeat to the white sauce (making sure there are no bones or shell) and transfer to individual ovenproof dishes. Top with the grated cheese and mushrooms and place in a fairly hot (225°) oven or under a griller until the cheese has melted and is beginning to turn brown.

This dish may be served as an entree or a main course. The above quantities are adequate for six reasonable servings.

PRAWNS IN A COCONUT

1 kg prawns
6 small green coconuts
100g butter
2 tablespoons cornflour
1 litre coconut milk
150ml of Pernod
salt, pepper
a liberal dash of cayenne

Cut the top off the coconuts with a hacksaw or sharp knife and empty out the water.

Shell and devein the prawns.

Prepare a basic white sauce from the butter, flour, coconut milk (from mature nuts, of course) salt and pepper (see above), and add the cayenne and Pernod. Mix well and then add the prawns. Fill the coconuts with this mixture and put their tops back on, sealing them with a little cornflour and water paste. Cook in a 175° oven for about 45 minutes.

Serve with baked yam (see recipe p.150).

Crabmeat, lobster or fish may be substituted for the prawns.

CURRIED TROPICAL FRUIT AND CHICKEN

500g rice
1 litre chicken stock
500ml coconut milk
100g cornflour
1 teaspoon salt
1½ teaspoons curry powder
100ml cold water
juice of 1 lime
1 medium avocado, cubed
1 to 2 bananas, cut into slices
1 cup cubed pawpaw
1 cup cubed mango
1 cup cubed pineapple
3 cups cubed cooked chicken
3 coconut shells, halved (optional)

Traditionally this recipe calls for chicken; however, wild duck is a good alternative. Boil the chicken and keep the stock. Cook the rice in the chicken stock. Bring the coconut milk and 400ml of stock to the boil and add cornflour, salt, and curry powder that has first been mixed with the cold water. Stir constantly until thickened. Sprinkle lime juice over the avocado and banana. Toss with the other fruits and the chicken. Line 6 half coconut shells with rice and place a serving of the fruit-chicken mixture on top. Spoon over the curry sauce.

The fruit mixture should be at room temperature, and the rice and sauce hot. This may also be served in a large serving dish.

After a recipe by A.L. Crawford.

BAKED BREADFRUIT

1 medium sized breadfruit (allow half a breadfruit per person)
250g minced topside (or a tin of corned beef)
2 medium sized onions
4 cloves garlic
2 birdseye chillies
2 tablespoons tomato paste
2 tablespoons vegetable oil
salt, pepper
50g grated cheese (parmesan for preference)

Cut the breadfruit in half lengthways and scoop out about 0.5cm of the flesh and set aside.

Heat the oil and add the finely chopped onions, crushed garlic and crushed chillies. When the onions begin to brown, add the meat, tomato paste, salt, pepper and the breadfruit flesh. Mix well and simmer until the meat is cooked. Put the mixture in the breadfruit shells and cover with the grated cheese. Place the shells in a baking dish, to which a little boiling water has been added, and heat in a 150° oven until the cheese has melted and begins to turn brown (about 30 minutes).

With slight modification, this recipe can be used for pumpkin, pawpaw (see p.140), choko and eggplant. The filling can also be varied - for example, try breadcrumbs and tomato, crabmeat, or a prawn filling.

PORK MARITA

based on traditional highland cooking

1 *marita* (pandanus) fruit (see p.94)
pork (any cut will do; I prefer lean loin chops; allow 2 chops per person)
water
salt, pepper

Take one *marita* fruit, red or yellow. Cut it into sections of about 5-10cm for easy cooking, and boil in salted water. (I use about 1-1½ litres of water per 5kg of the fruit.) After about 20 minutes you should be able to easily remove the small red or yellow segments from the central pith, by scraping with a fork. Discard the pith and cook for another 10 minutes or so. Mash the mixture around a little with a fork to get as much of the 'grease' as possible off the hard kernels, and then strain the mixture through a coarse strainer. You will get a thick, oily sauce about the consistency of tomato puree, and in the case of red *marita*, not unlike it in appearance. You will not need all this sauce for a single meal and the residue may be frozen.

Meanwhile, season the pork with salt and pepper and sear in a little oil or grease. When seared (about 10 minutes), add the *marita* sauce to the pan, cover and cook for about half an hour.

The *marita* has a distinctive, delicate flavour which complements that of pork. The sauce also goes well with chicken or beef.

BAKED PAWPAW

1 medium sized green pawpaw (allow half a pawpaw per person)
250g minced topside (or a tin of corned beef)
2 medium sized onions
4 cloves garlic
2 birdseye chillies
2 tablespoons tomato paste
2 tablespoons vegetable oil
salt, pepper
50g grated cheese (parmesan for preference)

Cut the pawpaw in half lengthways and remove the seeds. Then scoop out about 0.5cm of the flesh of the pawpaw and set aside.

Heat the oil and add the finely chopped onions, crushed garlic and crushed chillies. When the onions begin to brown, add the meat, tomato paste, salt, pepper and the pawpaw flesh. Mix well and simmer until the meat is cooked. Put the mixture in the pawpaw shells and cover with the grated cheese. Place the shells in a baking dish, to which a little boiling water has been added, and heat in a 150° oven until the cheese has melted and begins to turn brown (about 30 minutes.)

CHICKEN IN GALIP NUT SAUCE

Boil the chicken in the water for about 20 minutes. Save the chicken stock for another occasion.

Remove the skins from the *galip* nuts (this can be done easily by immersing the nuts for about 2 minutes in boiling water) and grind them to a paste with a mortar and pestle.

Crumb the bread (minus crusts) and soak in the milk for about 10 minutes. Then mash into a paste (or blend at high speed for about 20 seconds).

Heat the olive oil in a large frying pan. Add the finely chopped onion and crushed garlic and cook until the onion is soft, but not brown (about 5 minutes). Add the ground, or finely chopped chillies, the ground *galip* nuts and salt and pepper. Mix well and cook at low heat for about 5 minutes. Then add the annatto oil and the bread-milk paste and stir till you have a smooth thick sauce.

Add the chicken, ensuring that it is well covered with the sauce and the cheese. Cook until the cheese has melted and the chicken is heated through.

Traditionally this dish is served with boiled potatoes.

6 chicken breasts
1 litre water
150g shelled *galip* nuts
250g white bread
400ml milk
1 medium sized onion (about 100g)
2 cloves garlic
4 birdseye chillies
100ml olive oil
½ teaspoon annatto flavoured oil (see p.83)
3 tablespoons parmesan cheese
salt, pepper

From a Peruvian recipe

CHICKEN AND PITPIT CASSEROLE

Steam *pitpit* for about 15 minutes in a little salted water. Fry the sliced onions, crushed garlic and sliced mushrooms in about 20g butter until the onions are soft (about 5 minutes).

Make a white sauce with the rest of the butter, flour, milk, salt and pepper (see p.136). Add the fried onions, garlic and mushrooms, and the white wine.

Place the chicken and steamed *pitpit* inflorescences (without their sheaths) in a casserole dish and pour the white sauce mixture over them. Cover and cook in a 150° oven for about 1½ hours.

Serve with rice.

After a recipe of Jane Garnaut

6 chicken breasts
12-18 highland *pitpit (Saccharum edule)*
500g mushrooms
2 medium sized onions (total about 200g)
3 cloves garlic
70g butter
1 tablespoon cornflour
500ml milk
salt, pepper
150ml white wine

BEEF AND GINGER

- 500g lean beef (preferably rump or topside)
- 2 tablespoons sesame oil
- 8cm fresh ginger root
- 4 spring onions
- 100ml soy sauce
- 200ml sherry or white wine
- ½ teaspoon sugar
- ½ teaspoon ve-tsin (monosodium glutamate) powder
- 1 tablespoon cornflour

Cut the beef into thin strips and brown in the sesame oil. Add the ginger, cut in thin strips and cook for about 5 minutes at a medium heat. Add the soy sauce, most of the sherry, sugar and ve-tsin; stir well, then cover and cook for about 15 minutes. Finally, add the chopped spring onion and the cornflour, mixed with the rest of the sherry, and stir thoroughly. Cook on a low heat for a further 5 minutes or so.

Serve with rice.

TAPIOCA CAKES

Finely grate the raw tapioca, add salt and pepper, and form into round shapes about 1 centimetre thick. Sandwich together with a filling of cheese and chopped onion and fry in hot oil until golden brown.

The filling can be varied — for example, cheese and cooked bacon or ham, cheese and curry powder, cheese and tomato or chopped prawns.

tapioca (1 small tuber per person)
savoury filling
salt, pepper
oil for frying

SAVOURY FILLINGS
cooked bacon and cheese
chopped prawns
crabmeat
cheese and tomato

TAPIOCA BALLS

Prepare as for the above recipe, omitting the filling, and shape the mixture into small balls. Fry until golden brown.

These quantities are sufficient for two people.

SAGO GRUB SATE

3 doz sago grubs
water

PEANUT SAUCE:
150g ground freshly roasted peanuts *or* 150g peanut butter
4 to 6 birdseye chillies, finely chopped
1 clove garlic, crushed
1 stem lemon grass, chopped
1 tablespoon lime juice
2 tablespoons soy sauce
200ml coconut milk
salt

Steam the sago grubs for about 10 minutes. I prefer to remove the heads but this is not necessary.

Meanwhile combine all the sauce ingredients and heat, but do not boil.

Put the grubs on saté sticks (6 to a stick) and cover with half of the sauce. Grill over a charcoal fire or under an electric griller for about 5 minutes then turn over, cover with the rest of the sauce and grill for another 5 minutes.

Serve with rice. This is a very rich dish.

CURRY-ON-PATROL

1 tin meat
curry paste
water
rice

A well as tabasco, soy sauce and sesame oil, a useful companion on patrol is a jar of Bolst's or Patwe's *masala* paste, or other prepared concentrated curry paste.

To make a quick and easy curry, boil about a cupful of water (250ml) and add 2 or 3 tablespoons of curry paste. Mix carefully, then add a tin of meat or duck. Cook for about 10 minutes and serve with rice. (This is sufficient for 2 pretty hungry people.)

Optional extras, if you have them, include chopped onion or spring onion, chillies, a few green leaves, and coconut milk (if you add coconut milk use less water).

FLYING FOX WITH PRUNES, AND CREAM SAUCE

6 flying foxes
500g prunes
300ml white wine
salt, pepper
flour
50g butter
1 tablespoon red currant jelly
250ml thick cream

Remove the flesh from the flying foxes. To do this, either plunge the animals in boiling water for a while then skin them and remove the flesh from the bones, or roast the animals for a little while on an open fire, remove and when cool, break open down the backbone and remove the flesh from the skin.

Soak the prunes overnight in 250ml of the wine (a little more if the prunes are very dry). Before using, gently heat the prunes in the wine for about 10 minutes.

Season the flying fox meat with salt and pepper and roll in flour. Heat the butter and cook the meat on a low heat till brown. Add the rest of the wine, cover and cook for a further 20 minutes. Next add the juice from the prunes. Transfer the prunes themselves to a serving dish and keep warm in a low oven.

After the meat has cooked for another 10 minutes or so, and the juice reduced a little, remove the meat and place on the serving dish with the prunes.

To the sauce in the pan, now add the red currant jelly (cranberry sauce is not a bad substitute) and mix thoroughly. Then, a little at a time, add the cream to form a thick smooth sauce.

Pour this over the flying fox and prunes and serve.

After a New Caledonian recipe

MUMUED MUMUT

bandicoot
breadcrumbs (about half a large loaf)
onions
salt, pepper, herbs
butter.

Bandicoot is a popular bush food. The flesh is firm and white, and can be cooked like rabbit. The following is based on an Australian bush recipe.

Remove the entrails and either singe the animal over a fire or plunge it in boiling water, and then scrape off the fur. Clean the stomach cavity, fill it with stuffing made from breadcrumbs, onions, salt, pepper, herbs and a little butter, and close it (sew or use skewers). Cook in an earth oven for about 2 hours.

One large bandicoot is sufficient for about 3 or 4 people.

BAKED SNAKE

Snakes are not easy to cook and I do not profess to any great expertise. Frequently in Papua New Guinea, they are slowly smoked over a fire inside the house, and this seems to be as good a method of cooking as any.

The following recipe is an Australian bush recipe.

Heat the whole snake slowly over a fire, stretching it continuously; this ensures that the juices are retained without the snake contorting. Then make shallow incisions along both sides close to the backbone to cut the sinews. The snake may then be rolled up and tied like a rolled roast and baked in a low oven or on an open fire. The insides should be removed before serving.

The size of the serving, of course, depends on the snake.

CHICKEN CURRY

6 chicken breasts
2 medium sized onions (total about 200g)
10 *galip* nuts
1 tablespoon grated fresh ginger
10 birdseye chillies
1 stalk of lemon grass
3 tablespoons crushed coriander seeds
1 teaspoon cumin
1 teaspoon fennel
1 teaspoon cinnamon
1 teaspoon turmeric
3 cloves garlic
¼ teaspoon shrimp paste
50ml vegetable oil
milk of 1 (large) coconut

Heat the oil in a pan and when hot add the onions, finely chopped; *galip* nuts, thickly sliced; ginger, finely grated; chillies, crushed; lemon grass finely chopped; shrimp paste, and all the spices. Cook for about 3 to 4 minutes then add a little coconut milk and mix into a paste. Add the chicken and stir well to ensure it is covered with paste. Then add half the remaining coconut milk, cover and cook gently until the chicken is cooked (about 25 minutes). Shortly before serving add the rest of the coconut milk.

This dish can be made beforehand and reheated.

Served with rice.

Based on a Malaysian recipe

MAGANI STEW

1 small wallaby
about 100g flour
3 onions
salt, pepper
1 tablespoon juniper berries (optional)
other vegetables (optional)

Lightly cooked wallabies are fairly readily available in Port Moresby markets. Cut the meat off and into small cubes. Roll them in flour, salt and pepper. Put in a pot or casserole dish and add the onions, sliced, and juniper berries if you have them. Other vegetables, such as taro and carrots, may be added at this stage. (Sweet potato is not a good vegetable to use; it cooks up too much.)

Cover liberally with water. Cook with a lid on, on a low fire or in a 175° oven for about 2½ hours.

STUFFED TARO LEAVES

Mix the boiled rice, meat, finely chopped onion, thinly sliced ginger, salt, pepper and coconut cream. Place about 2 to 3 tablespoons of the mixture on each taro leaf and fold the leaf around it to form a neat package, which can be secured by tying or by skewers. Bake in a low (150°) oven for about 20 minutes.

250g boiled rice
1 medium sized onion (100g)
  or 3 spring onions
1 tin corned beef
ginger
salt, pepper
cream of 1 coconut
about 20 edible taro leaves

BAKED YAM

1 yam (allow half a medium sized yam per person)
50g butter
2 tablespoons milk
salt, pepper

Wash the yam but do not peel it. Bake in a 150° oven for about 45 minutes. Remove it from the oven and when it is cool enough to handle, cut in half and scoop out most of the yam, retaining the shell. Mash the yam thoroughly with the butter, milk, salt and pepper.

Put the mixture in the yam shells (if desired, sprinkle with grated cheese) and return to the oven. Cook for another 20 minutes or so.

BAKED TARO

Peel the taro (see p.107 on peeling taro) and cut into thin slices. Grease a wide casserole dish with the butter and place the sliced taro in it. Add the salt, pepper, chopped chillies and pour the coconut milk over the top. Cover the dish and cook in 175° oven for about 1½ hours.

Take the dish from the oven, remove the lid and sprinkle the grated cheese on top. Then return it, uncovered, and bake until the cheese is golden brown.

2 medium sized taro (total about 1kg)
10g butter
milk of one coconut
salt, pepper freshly ground black
2 birdseye chillies
50g grated cheese

TARO CAKES

1 medium sized taro (about 500g)
1 tablespoon milk (or coconut milk)
20g butter
1 egg yolk
salt, pepper
flour
vegetable oil

Peel the taro (see p.107 on peeling taro) boil and mash it; mix in the milk, butter, egg yolk, salt and pepper, and shape into flat cakes. Roll these in flour and fry in oil. 500g of taro will yield about a dozen small cakes.

KAUKAU CASSEROLE

Parboil the sweet potatoes and cut into round slices. Place the rounds in layers in a casserole dish. Between each layer place thin slices of butter, brown sugar, salt and pepper. Pour the orange juice over the lot. Bake, covered, in a 150°C oven for about 30 minutes and then uncovered for 5 minutes.

This dish goes well with pork and chicken.

Southern U.S.A.

500g sweet potato
100g butter
200ml. orange juice
6 tablespoons brown sugar
salt and pepper

BREADFRUIT AND CHEESE BAKE

1 breadfruit
4-6 rashers of bacon
1 large onion
3 large ripe tomatoes
2 tablespoons parsley
salt, pepper
100g grated tasty cheese

Bake the breadfruit in a 150° oven until tender - a skewer should pass easily through the skin. (This could take up to an hour depending on its size.)

Meanwhile fry the bacon in its own fat until brown. Remove from the pan and fry the diced onion in the bacon fat, together with the chopped tomatoes, until browned. Mix together the bacon, onion and tomato mixture, salt, pepper and parsley.

Dice the flesh from the breadfruit and place half the amount in a greased ovenproof dish. Spread half the bacon mixture over this, together with half the grated cheese. Repeat with remaining ingredients.

Bake in a 150° oven for approximately 30 minutes, or until the cheese is nicely browned.

After a recipe by J.A. Crawford.

GRILLED PITPIT

Strip the outside sheath to reveal the inflorescence itself. Slice the bud in half lengthways and place on the griller. Smother with lime juice and dot with butter. Cook under a medium griller until golden brown.

If so desired, the cooked *pitpit* can be served in a shallow dish with a simple white butter sauce.

6 *pitpit (Saccharum edule* inflorescences)
lime juice
50g butter
white butter sauce (optional)

SWEET POTATO SOUFFLE

500g sweet potato
50g butter (plus a little extra for greasing the souffle dish)
200ml milk
50g grated cheese
2 egg yolks
3 egg whites
salt, pepper

Boil the sweet potatoes, peel and mash. Slowly add the butter, milk, half the cheese, egg yolks, salt and pepper. Set the mixture aside to cool.

Separately, beat the egg whites until stiff. When the sweet potato mixture has cooled to about room temperature, fold in the egg whites.

Transfer the souffle mixture to the souffle dish (1 litre capacity) which has been well greased with butter, sprinkle the rest of the cheese on top and bake in a 175° oven for about 30 minutes. When the souffle has risen and the top is golden brown, remove from the oven and serve immediately.

VEGETABLES IN COCONUT MILK

This dish is the usual meal of the majority of lowlands people.

Preferably it should be prepared in a clay pot on an open fire. To prevent vegetables sticking to the bottom of the pot, line with banana leaves or place a couple of green twigs at the bottom of the pot.

Peel the vegetables and place in the pot, with the denser vegetables (such as taro, yam and some cooking bananas) near the bottom. Barely cover with salted water, add greens, and cover the pot with leaves or a half coconut shell. Cook till the tubers are ready to eat. Before serving add the coconut milk and remove from the fire.

Eat the vegetables and drink the broth.

Vegetables (sweet potato, taro, yam, tapioca, pumpkin, banana...)
leafy greens (any greens - see chapter three)
water
salt
coconut milk

BEANS IN COCONUT

500g beans (pods)
1 small onion
3 cloves garlic
2 birdseye chillies
50g grated coconut
1 tablespoon ghee or vegetable oil
salt

Slice the beans and lightly steam in a little salted water until tender (about 10 minutes).

Fry the chopped onion, crushed garlic and chopped chilli until the onion begins to brown. Add the coconut and beans and more salt, if needed, and cook for another 3 or 4 minutes.

South Indian recipe

YAM PUDDING

Cook the yam, discard the skin, and mash the vegetable with the salt and pepper and, if necessary, a little water or milk so that you have a mash with the consistency of a stiff dough. Form the 'dough' into a bowl shape, place the filling in the middle and then close up the top. (A pie dish may be used to provide a more conventional shape - see photograph.)

Wrap in banana leaves and cook in an earth oven, or cook in foil in a 175° oven for about 1 hour. The yam casing should form a hard outside crust.

If you like, before serving, open the top and pour in coconut cream.

These quantitites are sufficient for two people.

1 medium sized yam (about 500g)
salt, pepper
250g of filling
coconut cream (optional)

SUGGESTED FILLINGS
chopped prawns
tinned meat
onions and chilli
fish and greens
aubergine
garlic and tomato
choko and grated cheese

PEANUT CAKES

sweet potato
roasted peanuts
coconut
salt
egg or flour

Cook and mash the sweet potato. Grind the roasted peanuts into a fine meal. Blend the two in equal proportions and add grated coconut and salt to taste. Add a little coconut cream to moisten the mixture and use egg or flour to bind it. (One egg or about 50g of flour will bind about 1kg of sweet potato and peanut.)

Make into flat cakes and fry or bake.

UBAI

Adzera cooking, Morobe Province

tapioca
coconut (or other filling)
salt
banana leaves (for cooking)

FILLINGS
boiled greens
tinned meat or fish
mashed banana
grated pineapple

Finely grate sweet tapioca tubers. Place the grated tapioca thinly on rectangles of banana leaf about 20cm long, sprinkle with salt. On top of this, down the centre, place grated coconut or other filling; then roll the banana leaf and secure the ends, so that the tapioca encloses the coconut like a filled pancake. Tie the bundle with strips taken from the centre of the banana leaf, and place over hot ashes for about 20 minutes, turning to ensure even heating.

I have tried cooking in aluminium foil under a griller, but the results were not comparable with those of cooking over an open fire.

When cooked remove the charred banana leaf. The tapioca, with its high starch content, will have blended together, enclosing the coconut, and you will have something which looks a little like a spring roll and tastes excellent.

Ubai may be served as a savory or a sweet dish.

One 500g tuber will make about two *ubai*

PITPIT AND HOLLANDAISE SAUCE

pitpit

HOLLANDAISE SAUCE
(sufficient for about 20 *pitpit*)
250g butter
3 egg yolks
1 tablespoon cold water
1 tablespoon lemon or lime juice
salt and pepper

This dish may be made using either of the two *pitpits* (see p.80). They are cooked similarly. I prefer to use the highland *pitpit Setaria palmifolia.*

For *Setaria*, strip the tough, hairy outside leaves (especially near the top) and steam or bake for about 30 minutes. After cooking it is not a bad idea to strip off another layer or two. Lay the cooked shoots neatly, like asparagus, on a serving dish and cover with Hollandaise sauce.

To make Hollandaise sauce:
Whisk the egg yolks until they thicken (about a minute), then add the water, lemon juice and salt and whisk again until all the ingredients are blended. Place in a heavy saucepan or, preferably, a double boiler. Meanwhile, gently melt all but about 25g of butter and set aside. Add the unmelted butter to the mixture and heat very slowly, whisking continuously, until you have a smooth thick cream. (This must be done very carefully; sudden heat will cause the mixture to curdle and excessive heat will give you scrambled eggs.) Add the melted butter, very slowly, while continuing to whisk gently. The sauce should be thick and creamy. When all the butter is integrated add the pepper and more salt or lemon juice if necessary.

For an entree allow 3 or 4 *pitpit* per person.

CREAMED BREADFRUIT

1 breadfruit (about 1kg)
20g butter
100ml milk (or coconut milk)
1 egg
salt, pepper

Boil the breadfruit until it is soft (about 30 minutes), and when cool, remove the skin and any seeds. Mash the flesh together with the butter, salt and pepper, and slowly add the milk and egg, beating thoroughly. Place in an ovenproof dish and bake at about 175° until brown on top.

HASBIN SALAD

hasbin seeds
vinaigrette dressing (oil, lemon juice, salt and garlic)
parsley or *Oenanthe javanica*

Remove the red seeds from the *hasbin* pods; do not cook. Add vinaigrette dressing and a little chopped parsley or *Oenanthe javanica.*

GUACAMOLE

1 large avocado
2 medium sized tomatoes
1 medium sized onion
fresh coriander (leaf)
3 birdseye chillies
juice of 1 lime
salt, pepper
2 cloves garlic (optional)

Guacamole is almost a staple in Latin America, where it is eaten with tortilla dishes, refried beans and just about anything else. Ingredients are variable, except perhaps for the avocado, tomato and onion.

Remove the flesh of the avocado and mash with the tomatoes, finely chopped onion and other ingredients. Serve as cold as a dip or (if you do not mind mixing ethnicities) as a side dish with curries, fried chicken and fried fish.

Mexican recipe

AVOCADO DIP, LEBANESE STYLE

1 large avocado
2 cloves garlic
juice of one lime
2 rashers bacon

Fry the bacon till it is crisp and when it has cooled, crumble it into very small pieces.

Remove the flesh from the avocado and mash with the crushed garlic, lime juice and bacon.

Serve as for guacamole.

FRIED GREENS

leafy greens
lime juice
water
butter (or oil)
garlic
salt, pepper

Lightly steam the greens in a little salt water and a squeeze of lime juice. Any greens will do: I prefer amaranth, water *kaukau* and *tulip*. Cook for about 5 minutes. Meanwhile crush or finely slice some garlic and heat it in a little butter or oil. Drain the greens, add the pepper and fry in the garlic flavoured oil for about 5 minutes.

The greens reduce drastically with cooking. One 20 toea bunch of greens is barely sufficient for two people.

PAWPAW SHERBET

1 medium sized pawpaw (about 500g)
100g sugar
250ml water
pinch of salt
2 egg whites
2 tablespoons lime juice

Peel the pawpaw, remove the seeds and mash the pulp.

Boil the water, sugar, lime juice and salt until it begins to form a thin syrup (about 5 minutes) then allow to cool.

Beat the egg whites until stiff, and when the syrup is cool, add them slowly to the syrup, beating continuously. Then add the pawpaw pulp.

Place in an ice cream tray (or two) and freeze for about 2 hours, stirring each half hour to break up the ice particles as they form.

PAWPAW SOUFFLÉ

- 1 medium sized pawpaw (about 500g)
- 150ml water
- 50ml lime juice
- 100g sugar
- 2 tablespoons cornflour (or tapioca flour)
- 2 eggs

Peel the pawpaw, remove the seeds and mash the pulp, then heat it together with the water and all but 1 tablespoon of the sugar, until the mixture boils.

Mix the flour with the lime juice and add it to the pawpaw. Stir over a low heat until the mixture thickens; then add the egg yolks. Remove from the heat.

When the mixture is nearly cool, beat the egg whites with the remaining sugar until just stiff, and fold into the mixture.

At this point the soufflé may be either frozen or cooked, as for a normal soufflé, in a 175° oven until it has risen (about 25 minutes).

MANGO MOUSSE

12 ripe mangoes
500ml cream
2 tablespoons sugar

Remove the flesh from the mangoes and put it, together with the sugar and cream, into a blender. Blend for about 20 seconds at high speed and freeze for at least 2 hours. This is a much less complex recipe than many I have seen, but it gives good results.

MANGO SHERBET

3 mangoes
4 tablespoons lime juice
50g sugar
250ml water

Pour the boiling water over the sugar, stir until the sugar is dissolved, and then cook at a fairly high heat for about 5 minutes until you have a light syrup. Put aside to cool.

Prepare a puree from the mango flesh (put the flesh in a blender for 30 seconds or so, or push it through a strainer) and add the lime juice.

Combine the syrup with the puree in an ice cream tray and freeze for about 4 hours, stirring every half hour to break up the ice particles as they form. Sherbet should have a fluffy, snowy texture.

Pawpaw or pineapple may be substituted for mango.

LIME CUSTARD FREEZE

6 egg yolks
250g sugar
200ml evaporated milk
10g gelatine
2 tablespoons water
200ml lime juice
4 egg whites

Place the egg yolks and sugar in a bowl, and whisk until the two are combined in a thick cream. Heat the milk to just below boiling and slowly add the egg yolks, whisking continually. Transfer the mixture to a saucepan and heat till you have a light custard (keep the heat moderate; if it is too hot the custard may curdle).

Meanwhile dissolve the gelatine in 2 tablespoons of boiling water and add the lime juice.

Add the gelatine and lime juice to the custard, and place in a bowl to cool.

Beat the egg whites until stiff and when the lime custard is cool, fold the two together and freeze for about 3 hours.

AVOCADO ICE CREAM

3 avocados (about 600g)
400g sugar
450ml coconut milk
juice of two limes
a large pinch of salt

Mix the avocado flesh and other ingredients carefully and freeze.

SOURSOP ICE CREAM

1 soursop (about 1kg)
10g gelatine
150ml water
150g sugar
250ml evaporated milk

Extract the pulp from the soursop, removing the seeds. Heat the water and add to the gelatine and sugar. Stir until dissolved and let cool. Add the soursop pulp.

Beat the evaporated milk until it is thick, then fold it into the gelatine and soursop mixture.

Place in an ice cream tray (you may need two) and freeze for about 3 hours stirring a couple of times to break up the ice particles as they form to ensure a smooth consistency.

BANANAS FLAMBÉ

6 ripe bananas
50g butter
100g brown sugar
2 tablespoons coriander
100ml Strega liqueur

Heat the butter in a pan. Peel the bananas and slice lengthways. Place in the pan and cover with the brown sugar and coriander. Cook on medium heat until soft (about 5 minutes) turning once. Warm the liqueur gently in a separate pan, pour over the bananas and ignite.

When serving,lift the bananas out carefully with an egg slice so that they do not break, and cover with the sauce.

An alternative is to take 2 ripe bananas for each person, peel and halve lengthways and place in a shallow fireproof dish. Sprinkle with lime or lemon juice, sugar and cinnamon, and dot liberally with butter. Place under a medium griller, and when soft and golden, bring to the table and pour over about 600mls of brandy and ignite.

Serve with ice cream or fresh cream, or both, and cover with the sauce.

PUMPKIN PIE

To make the pastry, cut the butter into the flour until it is in pieces about the size of a pea. Rub the butter into the flour with the fingers. Add the water and mix the dough thoroughly by hand. Roll the dough out on a floured board and, finally, use it to line a 20cm pie dish.

Peel the pumpkin and remove the seeds. Boil it and discard the water. Mash the boiled pumpkin and add to it the melted butter, beaten eggs, molasses, sugar, flour, milk, salt and spices. Mix thoroughly.

Fill the pie casing with the pumpkin mixture and bake in a moderate (175°) oven for an hour.

Serve hot or cold with (or without) cream.

U.S.A. recipe

PIE SHELL
100g plain flour (plus a little in which to roll the pastry dough)
2 tablespoons cold butter
3 tablespoons cold water
pinch of salt

FILLING
1 small pumpkin (about 500g)
2 eggs
30g butter
50ml molasses or golden syrup
200g sugar
1 tablespoon cornflour
½ teaspoon cinnamon
½ teaspoon nutmeg
½ teaspoon ground ginger
¼ teaspoon ground cloves
100ml milk
salt

SAGO-BANANA DUMPLINGS

6 eating bananas
250g sago flour
cream of one coconut

Mash the bananas and add the sago flour. Roll into balls. Drop the balls into boiling water and cook for about 20 minutes.

Serve with coconut cream.

TAPIOCA PUDDING

1 large tapioca (about 400g)
3 tablespoons sugar
2 eggs
milk of one coconut
1 teaspoon vanilla (optional)
10g butter

Finely grate the tapioca and add the beaten eggs and sugar, coconut milk and vanilla. Mix thoroughly and place in a baking dish which has been greased with a little butter. Bake at 150° for about 30 minutes.

PINEAPPLE FOOL

Peel and cut the pineapple and put it in a blender at high speed for about 45 seconds.

Whip the cream until it begins to stiffen. Add the vanilla, and if the pineapple is a little tart, a tablespoon or more of sugar. Continue beating until the cream is stiff enough to form peaks.

Chill the two separately for about 45 minutes. Then fold the cream into the pineapple, integrating the two thoroughly, and serve.

Mango may be substituted for pineapple.

1 medium sized pineapple
250ml cream
½ teaspoon vanilla essence
sugar to taste

VAKA LOLO

Boil the taro in salt water and when it is cooked mash into a smooth paste.

Cook the coconut milk and the sugar together with the grated coconut till you have a thick golden syrup, *lolo* (be careful it does not burn).

Roll the taro paste into balls and cover with the *lolo* syrup.

Fijian recipe

500g taro
milk of 2 coconuts
1 tablespoon grated coconut
1 tablespoon sugar

MANGO UPSIDEDOWN CAKE

Cut the flesh off the mangoes and steep it in the lime juice.

Meanwhile prepare the cake mix: cream the butter (all except for a little to be used to grease the cake tin) and sugar and add the beaten egg. Sift the flour into the mixture and add the salt. Slowly add the milk, stirring continuously.

Thoroughly grease a deep cake tin with a little of the butter and then cover with the brown sugar. Add the mango. Pour the cake mix on top of this and bake for about an hour in a 175° oven.

When the cake is cooked, turn out of the tin and serve while hot, with cream or ice cream.

4 ripe mangoes
juice of two limes
100g brown sugar
100g butter
250g sugar
1 egg
250g self raising flour
100ml milk
pinch of salt

HIBISCUS JELLY

20g gelatine
1 litre water
4 tablespoons sugar
20 red hibiscus flowers

Pour all but about 100ml of the boiling water over the hibiscus flowers and add the sugar. Allow to steep for 5 to 10 minutes. Put the rest of the water in a cup and add the gelatine; stir till the gelatine is dissolved. Strain the water off the hibiscus and add to the gelatine in a jelly mould. Cool it, then refrigerate till the jelly is set. Hibiscus jelly has an attractive Tiffany pink hue and a delicate flavour.

COCONUT PASTRIES

Combine the grated coconut, flour and sugar and mix in the butter. Add the egg yolk and the coconut cream to make a soft dough. Knead on a floured board. Roll out till about 1cm thick and cut into biscuit size slices.

Place on a greased tray and bake at 175° for about 15 minutes.

Filipino recipe

50g grated coconut
100g self raising flour
1 egg yolk
20g butter
1 teaspoon sugar
150ml coconut cream
vegetable oil

CRYSTALLIZED PAWPAW FLOWERS

Gather the flowers, carefully, early in the morning. Prepare the syrup of sugar, water and lime juice (4 parts water, 3 parts sugar and one of lime juice). Drop the flowers in the boiling syrup and cook till they are translucent. Remove gently and allow to crystallize.

pawpaw flowers
sugar
lime juice
water

MARGARITA

3 parts tequila
1 part fresh lime juice
1 part Triple Sec or Cointreau
ice
salt

Mix the tequila, lime juice and Triple Sec. Serve on crushed ice in a salt rimmed glass. (To prepare the glass, moisten the rim with lime juice and dip it in a saucer of salt.)

PAWPAW AND MILK FRAPPÉ

1 medium sized ripe pawpaw (about 1kg)
100ml milk (or coconut milk)
50ml lime juice
50g sugar
½ teaspoon vanilla essence
1 cup crushed ice

Remove the skin and seeds from the pawpaw and slice it coarsely into a blender. Add all the ingredients and blend at high speed for about 30 seconds.

The quantities yield about a litre of thick frappé.

The addition of brandy does the mixture no harm.

Caribbean recipe.

SOURSOP SCHNAPPS

Extract the pulp from the soursop and add it, with the sugar, to the vodka.

Steep for about 4 weeks in a sealed bottle,shaking daily. Filter through a coffee filter and rebottle.

1 soursop - (about 1kg)
3 tablespoons sugar
750ml bottle vodka

COMFORTING COCONUT

Chill a green coconut. When chilled take a little slice off the top and empty out the water. Put the liqueur and the coconut milk into the coconut and then top up with the green coconut water. Drink through a straw. One coconut goes a long way.

100ml Southern Comfort liqueur
100ml coconut milk
green coconut water

COCONUT EGG FLIP

Combine the ingredients in a blender for about 20 seconds. For an alcoholic drink, add about 50ml of dark rum.

milk of 1 coconut
2 egg yolks
½ teaspoon vanilla essence

JAMAICAN COCONUT

Mix the brandy, Tia Maria and coconut milk. Serve on crushed ice.

1 part brandy
1 part Tia Maria liqueur
1 part coconut milk
ice

PINA COLADA

Mix the rum, pineapple and lime juice and, last, the coconut milk. Serve on crushed ice.

2 parts white rum
2 parts fresh pineapple juice
1 part lime juice
1 part coconut milk
ice

GEREGERE GROG

3 parts *geregere* syrup (see below)
2 parts dark rum
1 part lime juice
ice

PANDANUS SYRUP
ripe yellow segments of 1 coastal pandanus fruit (*geregere*) (see p.69)
100g sugar
1 litre water

To make the syrup, cook the fruit in the water and sugar, mashing a little once the fruit has softened, until you have extracted a good part of the pulp of the fruit. (This should take 15-20 minutes.) Cook a little longer till you have a thin syrup. Strain and bottle.

For the grog, combine the syrup, rum and lime juice and serve on crushed ice.

DAIQUIRI

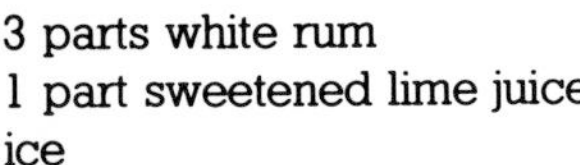

3 parts white rum
1 part sweetened lime juice
ice

Mix the rum and sweetened lime juice and pour over crushed ice.

For variation, substitute fivecorner juice for lime juice.

FURTHER READING

Although there has been no systematic study of food and its place in traditional society in Papua New Guinea, there are copious references to food in writings of travellers, anthropologists, geographers and others.

Among the more substantial and interesting accounts of traditional food are those contained in W.C. Clarke's *Place and People* (Australian National University Press, 1971), Bronislaw Malinowski's *Coral Gardens and their Magic* (George Allen and Unwin, 1935), R.A. Rappaport's *Pigs for the Ancestors* (Yale University Press, 1967), Marie Reay's *The Kuma* (Melbourne University Press, 1959), Eric Waddell's *The Mound Builders* (University of Washington Press, 1972), Michael Young's *Fighting with Food* (Cambridge University Press, 1971), Tony Crawford's *Aida, Life and Ceremony of the Gogodala* (Robert Brown & Associates, 1981), and a 1979 University of Queensland Ph.D. thesis, *Wopkaimin Subsistence* by D. Hyndman. David Lea has written specifically on yam growing in the Maprik area, in *Papua and New Guinea Agricultural Journal* (PNGAJ) vol. 18 no. 1, 1966, and Patricia Townsend on sago production in the upper Sepik, in *Human Ecology* vol. 2 no. 3 1974. *Agricultural Traditions of the Mount Hagen Area*, by Jocelyn Powell, A. Kulunga, R. Moge, C. Pono, F. Zimike and J. Golson (UPNG, Department of Geography Occasional Paper No. 12, 1975) presents perhaps the most exhaustive study of traditional food plants and their origins, and in Occasional Paper No.6 of the Australian National University's Development Studies Centre, John Connell gives a detailed account of hunting and gathering among the Siwai of Bougainville.

There is also some useful material in several recently published collections of papers ; K. Wilson and R.M. Bourke (eds), 1975 *Papua New Guinea Food Crops Conference Proceedings* (Department of Primary Industry, 1976); Bob Densley (ed), *Agriculture in the Economy. A Series of Review Papers* (Department of Primary Industry, no date [1978?]); B.A.C. Enyi and T. Varghese (eds), *Agriculture in the Tropics* (University of Papua New Guinea, 1977); Donald Denoon and Catherine Snowden (eds), *A History of Agriculture in Papua New Guinea. A Time to Plant and a Time to Uproot* (Institute of Papua New Guinea Studies, no date [1980?]).

Other important general references, not confined to Papua New Guinea, include *Food Plants of the South Seas* by E. Massal and Jacques Barrau (South Pacific Commission, 1956), Barrau's *Subsistence Agriculture in Melanesia* (Bernice P.

Bishop Museum, 1958), *Kulu, Kuru, Uru. Lexicon of names of food plants in the South Pacific* by C. Jardin (South Pacific Commission, 1974), Douglas Yen's monumental *The Sweet Potato and Oceania* (Bishop Museum Press, 1974), J.W. Purseglove, *Tropical Crops, Dicotyledons 1, 2* (1968), *Monocotyledons 1, 2* (1972) (Longmans), and H.A.P.C. Oomen and G.J.H. Grubben, *Tropical Leaf Vegetables in Human Nutrition* (Koningklijk Instituut voor de Tropen, Amsterdam, 1978). Less easy to come by, but extremely useful, is a little booklet prepared in 1943 by the Auckland Museum ('in response to the demand for information about emergency foods of the Solomons combat area') entitled *Food is Where You Find It.*

There is a growing literature on the prehistory of Papua New Guinea agriculture, the more important contributions to which include R.N.H. and Susan Bulmer in the *American Anthropologist* volume 66, special issue 1964; numerous papers by Jack Golson, including chapters in J. Winslow (ed), *The Melanesian Environment* (Australian National University Press, 1977), G. de G. Sieveking, I.H. Longworth and K.E. Wilson (eds) *Problems in Economic and Social Archaeology* (Duckworth, 1976), J. Allen, J. Golson and R. Jones (eds), *Sunda and Sahul* (Academic Press, 1977) and W.N. Gunson (ed), *The Changing Pacific* (Oxford University Press, 1978); G.P. Keleny in *PNGAJ* vol. 15, nos. 1 and 2, 1962; papers by Powell in *Search* vol. 1 no. 5, 1970, in Winslow (1977) and in K. Paijmans, (ed) *Vegetation of Papua New Guinea* (Australian National University Press, 1976); articles by J.B. Watson in *Ethnology* volumes 3 (1964), 4 (1965) and 7 (1968) and in *Oceania* vol. 38 no. 2, 1967; E. Waddell's article in *Pacific Viewpoint* vol. 13, no. 1, 1972; Yen's article in *Archaeology and Physical Anthropology in Oceania* vol. VIII No. 1, 1973; and Pamela Swadling's *Papua New Guinea's Prehistory: an introduction* (National Museum and Art Gallery, Port Moresby, 1981).

Among a number of interesting studies by nutritionists are the *Report of the New Guinea Nutrition Survey Expedition, 1947* (Government Printer, Sydney), H.A.P.C. Oomen and S.H. Malcolm, *Nutrition and the Papuan Child* (South Pacific Commission, 1958); Nancy Hitchcock's study in *New Guinea Research Bulletin* no. 14, 1967 and J. Lambert, *A Study of Nutritional Status and Economic Development in Chimbu District, from 1956 to 1975* (Public Health Department, Konedobu, 1975). A recent review of the literature on subsistence agriculture and nutrition in Papua New Guinea may be found in IASER Discussion Paper no. 42, 1982, by G.T. Harris. A manual on *Nutrition for Papua New Guinea* and a regular newsletter, *Nutrition and Devel-*

opment, may be obtained from the Nutrition Section, Department of Public Health.

The Lowlands Agricultural Experimental Station at Keravat, East New Britain, has published a number of useful bulletins on local crops and how to grow them.

Unfortunately there is not, for Papua New Guinea, any equivalent to I.H. Burkhill's invaluable *Dictionary of the Economic Products of the Malay Pensinsula* (first published by the Crown Agents for the Colonies in 1935) or W.H. Brown's *Useful Plants of the Philippines* (Bureau of Printing, Manila, 1946). But many of the plants listed in these two works occur in Papua New Guinea and both (especially Brown, which is illustrated) are useful guides to identifying plants in Papua New Guinea. There is, however, Straatman's very useful *Ethnobotanical Checklist* (mimeo, New Guinea Research Unit, no date), a similar list attached to an article by Lea in the *Report of a Symposium on Ecological Effects of Increasing Human Activities on Tropical and Sub Tropical Forest Ecosystems* (Australian Government Publishing Service, 1976), and a more complete list in Powell's contribution to Paijmans' *Vegetation of Papua New Guinea.* Other useful aids to the identification of edible plants include part 2 of *Forest Botany* (Training Manual for the Forestry College, volume 3) by J.J. Havel (Papua New Guinea Department of Forests, 1975); E.E. Henty and G.S. Pritchard's, *Weeds of New Guinea and their Control* (Botany Bulletin no. 11, Office of Forests, Division of Botany, 1979), and *Handbooks of the Flora of Papua New Guinea* (two volumes edited respectively by J.S. Womersley and E.E. Henty, Melbourne University Press, 1978, 1982). Since some of the wild plants occurring in Papua New Guinea also grow in Australia, A.B. and J.W. Cribbs' *Wild Food in Australia* (Collins, 1974) may also be helpful.

Betel nut chewing is discussed by B.G. Burton-Bradley in articles in the *Papua New Guinea Medical Journal* vol. 21 no. 3 1978 and vol. 23 no. 1 1980 and the *Canadian Journal of Psychiatry* vol. 24 no. 5 1979, and by several contributions to Mac Marshall (ed), *Through a Glass Darkly: Beer and Modernization in Papua New Guinea,* IASER Monograph 18, 1982. Crawford has recorded the contemporary practice of kava drinking among the Gogodala in *Aida*.

The role of the pig is discussed in a number of anthropological and other studies, notable amongst which are R. Feachem, in *Mankind* vol. 9 no. 1 1975; Rappaport's *Pigs for the Ancestors;* Andrew Strathern's *The Rope of Moka* (Cambridge University Press, 1971) and a paper by A.P. Vayda, A. Leeds and D.B. Smith in V.E. Garfield (ed), *Proceedings of the 1961 Annual Spring Meeting of the American Ethnological Society.*

Useful guides to the identification of indigenous animals are A. Ziegler's, *Guide to the Native Land Mammals of Northeast New Guinea* (Wau Ecology Institute, n.d.) and J.I. Menzies and Elizabeth Dennis, *Handbook of New Guinea Rodents* (Wau Ecology Institute, 1979). For the identification of fishes and shellfish there are Ian Munro's excellent *The Fishes of New Guinea* (D.A.S.F., 1967) Alan Hinton's *Guide to Shells of Papua New Guinea* (Robert Brown & Associates, n.d.) and W.O. Cernohorsky's *Marine Shells of the Pacific* (Pacific Publications, volume 1 1967, volume 2 1973). Accounts of fishing and hunting techniques may be found in B. Anell's *Contribution to the History of Fishing in the South Seas* (Uppsala, 1955) and *Hunting and Trapping Methods in Australia and Oceania* (Lund, 1960), and an article by R. Bulmer in *Oceania* vol. 38, 1967-68.

The *Encyclopaedia of Papua New Guinea* (P. Ryan (ed), Melbourne University Press in association with UPNG, 1972) contains a good deal of information on food, especially in the entries of Agriculture; indigenous (by Lea), Ethnobotany (Yen), Fishing (B.A.L. Cranstone), Food (Margaret McArthur), Hunting (Bulmer), Marsupials (H.M. van Deusen), Molluscs (D.G. McMichael) and Pigs (Vayda).

APPENDIX

COMPOSITION OF COMMON FOODS

(Based on edible portions of raw foodstuffs)

	Source of information see p.188	Kilojoules per 100g	Protein %	Fat %	Carbo-hydrate %
TUBERS & STARCHES					
Sweet potato, white	1	378	0.4	0.1	22
Sweet potato, yellow	1	588	2.1	0.1	34
Taro (*Colocasia* sp.)	1	441	2.0	0.2	25
Taro (*Cyrtosperma* sp.)	1	588	0.8	0.5	33
Taro (*Xanthosoma* sp.)	1	567	2.0	0.5	30
Yam (*D. alata*)	1	399	1.2	0.1	23
Tapioca	1	546	0.8	0.3	30
Sago	1	1197	0.2	0	71
GREEN LEAVES & SHOOTS					
H. manihot	2	197.4	5.7	0.3	9
Amaranth	1	189	3.0	0.5	7
Tulip	1	378	5.9	2.2	12
Water *kaukau*	1	126	4.0	0.5	3
Pumpkin sprouts	3	109.2	3.8	n.d.	n.d.
Taro leaves (*Colocasia* sp.)	1	210	2.5	2.0	5
Sweet potato leaves	1	168	3.5	0.5	8
Tapioca leaves	1	315	6.2	1.0	10
Pawpaw leaves	1	378	3.0	2.0	15
Tree fern (*Alsophila* sp.)	3	180.6	5.5	n.d.	n.d.

Ascorbic Acid mg per 100g	Iron mg per 100g	Carotene mg per 100g	Thiamine mg per 100g	Riboflavin mg per 100g	Niacin mg per 100g	Calcium mg per 100g
60	0.6	0.035	0.08	0.05	0.4	20
70	0.6	1.000	0.15	0.05	0.8	40
6	1.0	0	0.10	0.04	1.0	15
n.d.	n.d.	n.d.	n.d.	n.d.	n.d.	n.d.
10	0.7	0.003	0.15	0.04	0.7	8
15	0.5	n.d.	0.10	0.03	0.5	15
35	0.5	n.d.	0.04	0.02	0.6	10
0	0.7	n.d.	0	n.d.	n.d.	30
n.d.	n.d.	n.d.	n.d.	n.d.	n.d.	580
70	30.0	5.850	0.01	0.25	1.3	300
200	2.7	10.275	0.10	0.33	1.5	330
60	4.5	2.465	0.12	0.27	1.6	50
18	3.0	n.d.	0.15	n.d.	n.d.	80
160	n.d.	7.500	0.20	0.50	3.0	400
25	8.0	3.600	0.10	0.20	0.9	70
300	2.0	0.090	0.12	0.30	1.7	175
200	0.8	10.950	0.16	0.90	2.1	350
26	n.d.	n.d.	0.15	n.d.	n.d.	n.d.

	Source of information see p.188	Kilojoules per 100g	Protein %	Fat %	Carb hydra %
GREEN LEAVES AND SHOOTS					
Water cress	1	63	2.4	0.2	1
Wild mulberry leaves	3	239.4	2.9	n.d.	n.d.
Pigweed	3	88.2	1.7	n.d.	n.d.
Pitpit (*S. palmifolia*)	2	113.4	0.5	0.2	7
Palm hearts (*Archontophoenix* sp.)	3	79.8	1.9	n.d.	n.d.
Bamboo shoots	2	113.4	2.6	0.3	5
CUCURBITS AND LEGUMES					
Pumpkin	2	138.6	1.3	0.3	8
Cucumber	2	54.6	0.8	0.1	3
Choko	3	33.6	0.2	n.d.	n.d.
Bitter melon	2	92.4	0.9	0.4	5
Wing bean, dried (*hasbin*)	2	1675.8	33.0	16.0	37
Hyacinth bean, dried	2	1419.6	22.2	1.5	61
Lima bean, dried	2	1419.6	20.0	1.5	63
Peanut	2	2293.2	25.6	43.3	23
NUTS & FRUIT					
Coconut meat, mature nut	2	1474.2	4.2	34.0	13
Coconut meat, immature nut	2	756	4.0	15	10
Coconut milk, mature nut	2	1306.2	2.5	34	5
Coconut water, immature nut	2	71.4	0.2	0.4	4
Pandanus (*karuka*)	2	2868.6	11.9	66.0	22
Polynesian chestnut	1	1008	4.5	4.5	40

Ascorbic Acid mg per 100g	Iron mg per 100g	Carotene mg per 100g	Thiamine mg per 100g	Riboflavin mg per 100g	Niacin mg per 100g	Calcium mg per 100g
35	3.4	0.700	0.08	0.10	0.9	80
49	n.d.	n.d.	0.15	n.d.	n.d.	300
25	3.6	n.d.	0.03	n.d.	n.d.	103
n.d.	n.d.	n.d.	n.d.	n.d.	n.d.	21
14	n.d.	n.d.	n.d.	n.d.	n.d.	550
4	0.5	0.012	0.15	0.07	0.6	13
11	0.6	0.240	0.06	0.03	0.4	18
8	0.3	0	0.03	0.04	0.2	10
4	0.1	n.d.	0.05	n.d.	n.d.	3
55	0.9	0.200	0.06	0.03	0.03	3
. .	n.d.	n.d.	0.08	n.d.	n.d.	n.d.
n.d.	3.5	n.d.	0.62	0.20	2.3	88
. .	6.0	. .	0.5	0.14	1.5	90
. .	1.9	0.018	0.84	0.12	16.0	52
0	1.7	0	0.06	0.03	0.6	9
10	1.3	0.006	0.05	0.03	0.7	8
0	1.0	0	0.02	0.01	0.3	15
n.d.	n.d.	n.d.	0	n.d.	n.d.	30
n.d.	n.d.	n.d.	n.d.	0.36	n.d.	419
n.d.	n.d.	n.d.	n.d.	n.d.	n.d.	n.d.

	Source of information see p.188	Kilojoules per 100g	Protein %	Fat %	Carbo hydrat %
NUTS & FRUIT					
Galip nut	2	2704.8	14.2	68.5	6
Banana (*M. sapientum*)	1	441	1.3	0.1	25
Breadfruit	1	231	0.8	0.5	12
Breadfruit seeds	1	630	6.0	0.5	30
Fig (*F. carica*)	2	273	1.2	0.4	16
Mangrove fruit	1	315	2.5	0.3	16
Pawpaw green	1	105	0.5	0.1	6
Pawpaw ripe	1	168	0.5	0.1	9
Mango	1	294	1.5	0.2	16
Guava	2	289.8	1.0	0.4	17
Laulau (*S. malaccense*)	1	105	0.6	0.1	5
Custard apple	1	630	1.5	0.2	24
Soursop	1	294	0.9	0.2	16
Passionfruit (*P. edulis*)	1	294	1.5	2.0	15
Lime (*C. microcarpa*)	2	168	0.4	1.0	8
Raspberry (*Rubus* sp.)	1	231	1.0	0.2	12
Pineapple	1	252	0.5	0.2	14
Avocado	2	945	1.8	23.4	6
OTHER EDIBLE PLANTS					
Sugar cane (juice)	2	298.2	0.3	n.d.	18
Pitpit (*S. edule*)	2	155.4	4.1	0	8
Job's tears	1	588	15.0	7.0	60
Fungus (*Agaricus* sp.)	2	96.6	2.4	0.3	4

Ascorbic Acid mg per 100g	Iron mg per 100g	Carotene mg per100g	Thiamine mg per 100g	Riboflavin mg per 100g	Niacin mg per 100g	Calcium mg per 100g
. .	2.6	0.027	0.95	0.12	0.4	119
10	0.7	0.050	0.05	0.08	n.d.	8
25	0.8	0.004	0.10	0.50	0.5	30
n.d.	n.d.	n.d.	n.d.	n.d.	n.d.	60
2	0.6	0.048	0.06	0.05	0.5	54
n.d.	n.d.	n.d.	n.d.	n.d.	n.d.	n.d.
30	0.3	0.045	0.03	0.03	0.2	40
70	0.4	0.290	0.03	0.03	0.4	20
75	0.4	1.375	0.05	0.05	0.5	10
160	0.9	0.110	0.03	0.04	1.2	18
15	0.4	0.006	0.03	0.03	0.3	6
40	0.6	0.007	0.10	0.12	1.0	20
20	0.3	. .	0.09	0.06	0.7	20
25	n.d.	n.d.	0	0.12	1.9	9
45	0.8	0	0.02	0.01	0.2	18
15	1.5	0.010	0.03	0.03	0.9	25
20	0.1	0.016	0.08	0.03	0.2	18
10	0.9	0.200	0.10	0.44	1.5	15
0	2.0	. .	0.02	0.1	0	6
21	n.d.	n.d.	n.d.	n.d.	n.d.	10
n.d.	n.d.	n.d.	0.30	0.25	6.3	70
5	1.0	n.d.	0.10	0.44	4.9	9

	Source of information see p.188	Kilojoules per 100g	Protein %	Fat %	Carb hydr %
ANIMAL FOODS					
Molluscs	2	298.2	10.0	2.0	3
Crustaceans (lobster, crab)	2	394.8	18.0	1.5	2
Fish, fatty, saltwater	2	739.2	20	1.0	0
Fish, other, saltwater	2	436.8	19	2.5	0
Fish, freshwater (*Tilapia*)	2	449.4	17.5	4.1	0
Pork (medium fat)	2	1528.8	12.0	35.0	0
Turtle	2	344.4	16.0	1.0	2
Sago grub	2	760.2	6.1	13.1	9
Locust	2	562.8	20.0	6.0	0

SOURCES

1. F.E. Peters, *Chemical Composition of South Pacific Foods. An Annotated Bibliography.* South Pacific Commission Technical Paper no.100. Noumea 1957

2. World Health Organisation, Western Pacific Regional Office. Quoted from *Liklik Buk Bilong Kain Kain Samting.* Wirui Press Wewak 1976

3. L. Hamilton, 'Indigenous versus introduced vegetables in village dietary', *Papua and New Guinea Agricultural Journal* 10(2), October 1955.

Ascorbic Acid mg per 100g	Iron mg per 100g	Carotene mg per 100g	Thiamine mg per 100g	Riboflavin mg per 100g	Niacin mg per 100g	Calcium mg per 100g
. .	10.0	0.06	0.05	0.15	1.5	150
. .	5.0	. .	0.05	0.10	2.5	100
. .	1.2	0.03	0.08	0.21	2.7	38
. .	0.8	n.d.	0.06	0.08	2.2	28
0	0.1	0.03	0.03	0.10	4.2	77
0	6.5	0	0.58	0.14	3.1	6
n.d.	1.0	n.d.	0.2	0.5	3.0	100
n.d.	4.3	n.d.	0.08	0.43	2.4	461
n.d.	1.0	n.d.	n.d.	0.5	2.2	30

NOTES

1. Food composition varies with variety, soil and other growing conditions, etc. These figures should be regarded as only an approximate indication.

2. n.d. denotes no data available, not necessary nil

3. . . denotes 'trace only'

PHOTOGRAPHIC CREDITS

K. Briggs 139, 144
W.C. Clarke 152-154
A.L. Crawford 8, 10, 23, 24-28, 30, 32-34, 39, 59-61, 62-68, 70,71, 75,76, 79, 87-90, 101, 103-107, 114, plus recipe photographs on the following pages 116, 117, 119, 120, 122, 123, 127-129, 131-133, 137, 138, 140, 142, 143, 146, 149-160, 164, 165, 167-170, 172, 173
R. Damon 58
David Eastburn 41, 53, 54, 93
Anthony Forge 2, 42, 44, 45, 51
P. Gorecki 127
Institute of Papua New Guinea Studies 3, 16-19, 35-38, 91, 142, 155
K. Lagercrantz 4
M.A. MacKenzie 14, 73, 95, 134, 143
B.J. and M.R. Mennis 5, 157
Brian Miller 11-13, 49, 50, 128, 131, 149, 150
Office of Information, Papua New Guinea 136, 151
Margaret Tuckson 29, 46
Florence Weiss 9
Michael Young 15, 22, 120

All other photographs by R.J. and P.P May

INDEX